KW-222-654

Personal Use

by
the northlondonhippy

This book was first published electronically in
September 2016

This print edition was first published in November 2016

© Copyright 2016 "the northlondonhippy"

The moral right of this author has been asserted

ISBN Number: 978-1-326-77363-2

This book is dedicated to all the victims and casualties of the shameful, pointless 'War on Drugs'. You all deserve better. We all deserve better.

10% of all profits from this book will be donated to drug charities, annually.

Table of Contents

"You want to know something? We are still in the Dark Ages. The Dark Ages--they haven't ended yet."

— **Kurt Vonnegut, Deadeye Dick**

"One has a moral responsibility to disobey unjust laws."

— **Martin Luther King Jr., Letter from a Birmingham Jail**

Forward
35 Years On Drugs

Hello. I'm the northlondonhippy and I have a drug problem.

No, silly. Not that kind of problem!

My problem with drugs is this: The drug laws are stupid and the substances I enjoy most are prohibited by law.

More than that, they are the subject to the dumbest war in the history of all wars, the Drug War.

The war on drugs isn't really a war against drugs, it's a war against people who use some drugs. Nice people. Decent people. People like me. Maybe even people like you.

Chances are, someone you know, perhaps even someone you love, enjoys drugs too.

We are everywhere!

Don't worry, I am not a combatant in this pointless war, I'm a conscientious objector. And a make believe activist too. But that's OK, because I'm not really a hippy either, but I do portray one on the internet. Glad that's cleared up.

Drugs aren't really even illegal. How can you make a substance illegal?

15

What's prohibited is the possession of certain drugs. The act of possession is the illegal part.

If you have a pocketful of drugs, you are breaking the law. If the cops find a bag of drugs on the street, then there is no one to charge. They can confiscate them, but it's not a criminal matter, because there is no crime. The crime is having them in your possession. You need a human being in the equation for the laws to apply. Simple, eh? As if you needed proof it was a war on humans.

How can anyone be breaking the law, if the laws themselves are broken?

Drugs have been used as far back as recorded history goes, and probably even further. Altering our consciousness is about as human as it gets.

As a child, did you spin around madly and collapse on the ground from dizziness? Then you altered your consciousness. Groovy!

Do you drink alcohol? Smoke tobacco? Take caffeine? Eat sugar? Like a bit of chocolate? All of those legal substances affect your mood and brain chemistry. And they're all completely legal. And at least two of them are not good for your health. Guess which two?

The war on drugs has been a colossal failure. After spending billions over many decades, drugs are just as popular today as they have ever been. And stronger. And just as easy to get, perhaps in some ways, even easier.

Entire countries have been decimated because of the trade in drugs. I'm looking at you Mexico and Colombia. Countless lives have been lost and destroyed, because the effects of the laws are even worse than the drugs themselves.

A legal and regulated market would improve things dramatically, but there is misplaced resistance to taking a common sense approach. Drug law reform is long overdue.

Capitalism, at its most basic, is fairly simple. If there is a demand, a supply will find a way. And that is especially true for recreational drugs.

Alcohol prohibition didn't work, but it did create the Mafia. The drug trade is even bigger and yet we leave it in the hands of organised criminals, who make Al Capone look like a choir boy. Pablo Escobar was a very bad man, but no one had the choice of paying a little extra for organic, free trade cocaine. Under prohibition, there's only one brand in town, and that's the black market brand.

We don't regulate, we don't age check and we don't collect a single penny of tax on these very popular products. And that's just plain dumb.

If you're against a legal and regulated system of selling drugs, then you are against capitalism and no amount of protestations will convince me otherwise. I guess that makes you a Commie, you red bastard!

Unless you're profiting from the black market?

Or law enforcement? Or running a private prison? Shame on you if prohibition is part of your business model. It's state sponsored exploitation at its finest.

I've used drugs regularly and responsibly for over thirty-five years and my experiences have been over-whelmingly positive. I've mainly enjoyed cannabis, with a smattering of other substances thrown in for good measure.

In real life, I am a journalist and have worked for some of the largest news organisations in the world for the better part of the last 30 years. No one I know professionally, knows that I am the northlondonhippy, but just about everyone who knows me, knows I smoke weed. I've never hidden my love of the stuff. I've always done that intentionally, because there is an undeserved stigma attached to drug use.

It's time to smash that stigma into smithereens! Taking drugs is normal and millions of people have and will take them, every day.

There was a media campaign a few years ago, that had the tag line, "Nice people take drugs". I can confirm that's true. Nice people do take drugs. I'm nice and I take them frequently.

I grew up in the United States, where I saw first-hand the drug hysteria that was fuelled by the media and Nancy Reagan and her pointless 'Just Say No' campaign.

Anyway, it should have been 'Just say no, thank you'. Didn't anyone teach Mrs. Reagan manners? Wasn't she raised right? My mother taught me to always say 'please' and 'thank you'. Even drug dealers deserve your courtesy. Everyone does.

U.S. President Richard Milhous Nixon started the war on drugs way back in the 1970s, I remember that too. They were out to get the hippies and other minorities. No joke, one of Nixon's henchmen, John Ehrlichman, confirmed this was the reason for the war on drugs, during an interview conducted in 1994 that was recently published. It had nothing to do with the harms caused by drugs, it was just Tricky Dicky and his mates expanding the White House enemies list, exponentially.

Today, America is getting a bit more sensible about drugs and it's happening faster than I would have ever predicted. Around half of all US states have some sort of medical marijuana programme and a handful of states have legalised cannabis for recreational use, with many more expected to follow soon.

Entire countries are legalising cannabis too. Hello Uruguay, hello Canada. You guys rock!

With the largest prison population in the world, it is hardly a surprise that America is finally doing something. The drug laws really do cause more harm than the actual drugs ever could. Wars of this sort of duration are just not sustainable.

It's time to call a cease fire!

Cannabis is used medicinally by countless people around the world, including me. It can be used to treat a wide variety of ailments, from back pain to cancer, anxiety and depression, even AIDS.

Someone I know has been using cannabis as part of his drug cocktail to treat his HIV/AIDS for years. The prescription medication he takes, combination therapy, gives him all sorts of horrible side effects, including nausea. It also kills his appetite. Cannabis is the only drug that helps with these side effects and I have no doubt that without it my good friend would be dead. I'm glad he's not, I have enough dead friends already.

Why would anyone want to deny this lifesaving medication to someone in need? I don't have a good answer for that. No one does. There is simply is no good reason, just a lot of ridiculous and wrong ones.

Here in the UK, my adopted and permanent home, things are not really changing at all. Both major political parties ignore overwhelming evidence and common sense. They also ignore their government advisors.

A few years back, the government at the time shit-canned their chief drugs advisor, Professor David Nutt. Why? Because he dared to speak to the truth about drugs. Professor Nutt said cannabis and MDMA were safer than riding a horse, which is completely true, and he was crucified for it. Speaking the truth should be rewarded and praised, not punished.

It's the old free speech example. They say you can't shout 'fire' in a crowded theatre. That's bullshit. Of course you can, if its true. There's a moral obligation to always speak the truth. Professor Nutt did nothing wrong.

It's quite depressing to see stagnation on this important issue, in a country I love.

It wasn't always this bad. When Tony Blair was Prime Minister, he re-classified cannabis, from Class B to Class C. This was an encouraging and positive move that led me to believe that things were changing here for the better.

Then his successor, Gordon Brown, who was quite politically weak, reclassified it back to Class B, against the advice of his government advisors, to create the illusion he was a strong leader. It didn't work.

This was not a symbolic change, but a punitive one. The penalties for production and distribution are the same, be it Class B or C. The penalties for simple possession are far more severe for Class B substances. Nice. You can get 5 years in the big house for possession of one spliff. Does that seem just to anyone?

I did say it is a war against people, some of the most vulnerable people in our society. Prison should be for dangerous criminals that need to be kept away from society. Having a gram of weed doesn't make you dangerous, it makes you chilled. Right now, thousands of people are languishing in prison unnecessarily for possession of a plant. And, trust me, prison does them no favours. It seems like a foolishly high price to pay, just because you like to get high.

I like to get high.

I first tried cannabis in the late 1970s, but didn't really start smoking it properly until 1981, hence my 35 year designation. I still smoke it every day, and hope to continue to do so until I die. Or longer, if I can work out how.

As the world rediscovers cannabis and its many benefits, the lies forced down my throat and yours are slowly fading away. The truth will always win and the truth is that cannabis is "one of the safest therapeutically active substances known to man". I didn't say that, well I mean I did just type it, but the original source of that comment is Judge Francis Young, who was a US Drug Enforcement Agency Administrative Judge at the time, and he said this back in 1988.

Here's the full quote from Judge Young:

"In strict medical terms marijuana is far safer than many foods we commonly consume. For example, eating 10 raw potatoes can result in a toxic response. By comparison, it is physically impossible to eat enough marijuana to induce death. Marijuana in its natural form is one of the safest therapeutically active substances known to man."

I've written this book to help explain and normalise what it's like to be an unapologetic, long-term, prolific recreational drug user. I still have all my own teeth, I've been nearly continuously employed for my entire adult life and I've never stolen to fund my habits. I'm a decent, upright, tax-paying member of society, who just so happens to enjoy a spliff.

I've never been arrested or had any brushes with the law, but that could be because I am white, middle class(ish) and I've always been fairly cautious and careful. But I am mindful of the situation, I know that the risk of arrest is ever-present. And it shouldn't be. Arresting and imprisoning drug users is the epitome of stupidity. There is no compassion in our current drug policy.

And our prisons are awash with drugs. If you can't prevent the availability of drugs in a controlled and patrolled environment, how do you think you can stop them out here in the free world?

Spoiler alert: You can't.

Cannabis is safer than aspirin and that is a fact.

My source for that claim? Thirty-five years of my own personal use. Plus Professor Les Iversen, the current chairman of the UK government's Advisory Council on the Misuse of Drugs, said exactly that, back in 2000. It is just as true today, but no one in the UK government is listening.

It just has to change!

There's a terrible stigma that comes along with being a recreational drug user that is not deserved. I want to destroy that stigma. I want to consign it to history. I want everyone to realise that when you stigmatise a drug user, you are not doing them any favours, you are doing them a disservice. We all deserve better.

If all of this flies against everything you think you know about drugs, it's because everything you know about drugs is probably wrong. Don't worry, it's not your fault. You've all been lied to for decades.

It's time for the truth to win.

So let's kick this into high gear, as I take you on my thirty-five year journey of self-discovery through my rampant, prolific and joyous drug use.

the northlondonhippy
London, UK
21st September 2016

Chapter One
A Toe in the Water

Picture it, the late 1970s.

Hair was long, queues for petrol were even longer and disco music was king.

I was a dumb kid, living in a small beach town on the east coast of America.

Burt Reynolds was the biggest film star in the world, Jaws and Star Wars were immensely popular and the BeeGees were dominating the music charts.

The 70s were weird.

I went to a small high school, there were only 200 students in my year. I wasn't one of the cool kids, which I am sure will shock you. I wasn't one of the uncool kids either. I was just a kid, trying to figure out my place in the world.

I'm still trying to figure out my place in the world. Some things don't change.

The very first drug I experimented with was tobacco.

Legal, readily available and used by just about every adult I knew at the time, tobacco was the socially acceptable drug of choice for millions. Smoking was cool, smoking was popular, smoking was a favourite pastime for many people when I was a child. Smoking is also potentially fatal, but no one seemed to care back then.

Smokers today still don't.

Getting hold of cigarettes was easy, one of my friends acquired a pack of Marlboro Reds and a group of us went out into the woods near a local park. I was probably about 12 years old at the time. That would make it 1975.

We gathered in the woods, this small group of pre-teens, and we all lit up.

None of us really knew how to smoke, so we inhaled into our mouths and quickly exhaled. The unlucky amongst us, drew the thick smoke deeper into their lungs and were rewarded with convulsing coughs.

The taste was disgusting, but look how cool and grown up we all were! I wouldn't smoke a cigarette again for seven years. This experience was not enjoyable.

I started smoking cigarettes properly at the age of nineteen and didn't stop until a few years ago, at the tender age of fifty.

Cigarettes are stupid and I regretted getting hooked on them, but I still looked cool smoking them. Everyone does and that's one of the reasons why anti-smoking campaigns don't work. Smoking is cool, smoking is sexy. Emphysema and cancer, much less so, but they are decades away from your first smoke, so it's a hard sell.

These days, I am still hooked on nicotine, but I use an electronic cigarette, which is a much safer, healthier way to get that sweet nicotine buzz.

The next drug I experimented with was alcohol.

My parents, like the parents of all my friends, kept well-stocked bars in their homes, so we were all exposed to liquor at an early age. Booze was normal, acceptable and readily available, much like tobacco.

I used and abused liquor for years, but I don't drink any more.

I was 13 years old, the first time I got properly drunk. It was at a party at a friend's house.

I learned a couple of valuable lessons that night. One: that booze can make you sick. And two, if you swiped a small amount from every bottle in your parents' liquor cabinet, no one would notice.

Bug juice. That's what we called it. Bug juice. You would mix a small amount of every liquor in your parents' bar, into a bottle or jug, add something to kill the taste, like orange juice or fizzy pop and away you go.

One of the ingredients was always Creme de Menthe, a foul, minty mouthwash-like liqueur with a deep green colour. It was a popular gift, so everyone had a bottle of this, practically untouched. It became a staple ingredient in our bug juice. It always ensured a bright green colour that was the trademark of this foul swill.

A small group of us polished off a large pitcher of bug juice and proceeded to get loud and lairy. We went outside to smoke cigarettes and run around. That's what drunken 13 year-olds do.

At some point between going outside and getting collected by my parents, I realised I was unpleasantly drunk and a bit dizzy. And then I threw up and magically felt better.

I would repeat this routine on and off, for decades. Drink too much, throw up, and feel better.

As an adult, I drank like I meant it and could polish off copious amounts of spirits. Vodka, tequila and cognac were my favourites.

I stopped drinking completely, well, around 26 years later, in 2002. And I don't regret stopping at all, though it shocks me it took as long as it did to realise what a bad drug booze is. Live and learn. Eventually.

Tobacco and alcohol were part of my life, directly and indirectly, from my formative years right through to adulthood and middle age. And they are two of the worst drugs around in terms of harms to an individual and society.

While tobacco use has fallen, it still accounts for a shocking number of preventable deaths every year. And alcohol is one of the most damaging substances around, with many experts proclaiming it worse than heroin and cocaine due to the immense damage it continues to cause to individuals and society as a whole.

And it might have been the 1980s when the anti-drug hysteria reached its peak, but even back in the hippy-dippy 70s, the message was still clear: Drugs are bad, m'kay.

My mother was terrified by drugs, even though she was a heavy cigarette smoker and social drinker. She didn't see herself for the drug user she really was. She tried to pass this mixed message on to me, and it was surprisingly effective. I thought booze and cigarettes were acceptable, but drugs definitely not.

Only losers were users, I once thought. I couldn't have been more wrong.

My parents, like the parents of my friends, didn't discourage teenage drinking. In their view, drinking was OK, because 'at least it wasn't drugs'. Except it was a drug, but that distinction was lost on them back then. Just as it is now.

Alcohol and cigarettes are drugs, no doubt about that that, but they're legal, so that's OK. And they're deadly, which is also apparently just fine too.

Back then, keg parties were the done thing. Your parents would get half a keg of cheap beer and let you have your friends over. They enabled under-age drinking as a defence to drugs. Clever, eh?

At around the age of 16, I tried weed for the first time. I didn't get high, I didn't come even close, but the experience taught me a lot about my own fears and perceptions.

It was early evening, after school and post extra-curricular activities. I was invited to join a few of my friends on the school playing field, to sample the devil's weed for the very first time.

I remember being extremely nervous, worried that I would be out of control and stinking of dope, but I overcame my fears by asking my friends questions. What is it like? What does it taste like? Would people know immediately that I was high? They were all very reassuring.

We sat in a small circle, maybe half a dozen of us. A small, single skin joint was lit and passed around the circle. When my turn came, I really didn't know what to do, so I took a puff and passed it on. I coughed a lot and everyone laughed at the newbie.

I had several turns on the joint and I didn't feel any different. I had no idea how to smoke or how to get the smoke into my lungs. And I had no idea what I should be feeling, but I was fairly certain I wasn't feeling anything.

But I had finally tried weed and that was the main thing. I was part of a peer group, and my green cherry was well and truly popped… except I wasn't even slightly high.

They say weed doesn't make you paranoid, it's the illegality that does and that was certainly true for my first experience. I was absolutely terrified of being arrested, or worse my parents finding out I had dabbled in drugs.

We smoked another doobie, or rather my friends did, while I wasted more smoke and coughed. And when we were done, we all went home.

I remember walking into my house convinced my mother would take one look at me and know I was on drugs.

You don't just take drugs, or rather, once you take them, you are 'on drugs', presumably, for life.

I said a quick hello and went straight upstairs to my bedroom. I took off all my clothes, which I was convinced reeked of weed and stuffed them into a bag. I got dressed again in clean clothes and quietly took the bag of old, stinky weed-clothes out to the trash and threw my them away. Better to have one less outfit than have my shameful secret uncovered, now that I was 'on drugs'.

I didn't go back downstairs after that. I can remember, even now, lying in bed, in the dark, worrying about the risk I took. I wasn't even high, just scared.

Would I be craving acid next, or smack? Would I be stealing to support my new habit? Would I be grounded until I was 25, because I was dumb enough to take a few puffs from a joint only to end up 'on drugs'?

Of course not! But in my less than worldly wise, 16-year-old brain, a series of horrible outcomes awaited me.

Weed was very popular in my high school. This was the late 70s, in a beach town on the east coast of America. Weed was everywhere.

I remember watching a burnout surfer kid in one of my classes, rolling joints inside a textbook, our teacher completely oblivious to it. I saw kids, stoned out of their gourds, eyes red, lids drooping, attending other classes. And there were rumours about teachers, getting high in their cars before class. They were probably all true.

My brief brush with marijuana didn't put me off, exactly, but nor did it inspire me to try it again, at least not soon. I was still curious, but my curiosity was somewhat sated, because I could say with confidence that I had tried weed. I wouldn't smoke again for a couple of years.

In my senior year of high school, I fell in with a different group and they were proper, hardcore stoners. They were always high and while there was never any pressure to try it again, they certainly made it look more enjoyable.

They bought it by the quarter ounce, half ounce or ounce. It was what I would now call Mexican dirt weed: darkish brown, full of twigs and seeds and dry and dusty. This was known as commercial weed at the time. It came in by the plane or boatload, from south of the border. Some people called it Colombian Gold, but those in the know said it was from Mexico.

It never looked like much in the bag, that's for sure, nothing like the beautiful, manicured green buds we've grown accustom to today.

I observed the rituals of dope smoking, 1970s style. You would start with a gatefold, double album cover, opened and spread out in front of you. Led Zeppelin's Physical Graffiti was always a popular choice.

You would take the dirt weed and crumble it between your fingers on to the album cover, reducing it to dust. You would pull out the twigs and sticks, then sift with the edge of a pack of rolling papers, usually EZ-Widers, so the seeds would collect in the hinge of the album cover. You didn't want the seeds in your joint, as they would explode like popcorn with a loud snap.

Joints back then were thin, single skinners, rolled neat without tobacco. In America, we always smoked it neat, mixing with tobacco was something I would pick up when I moved to the UK and started smoking hash.

Headshops were everywhere, selling pipes, bongs, power hitters, doob-tubes, roach clips and any other bit of paraphernalia you can think of and more. My friends had a wide selection to try.

On the night of my high school graduation in 1981, I ended up at a pool party with my stoner friends. They were passing around joints, hitting bongs and generally having a very good time. We were also drinking.

One of my friends had a power hitter, a piece of paraphernalia that was popular at the time. It was a squeezee plastic bottle, with a screw cap on the end and a draw hole in the side. You unscrewed the cap, inserted a lit joint into the cap, then screwed it back on the bottle. When you squeezed the bottle while covering the draw hole, smoke was forced out the end of the cap in a steady, heavy stream. Hence putting the power into a power hitter.

My friends explained to me that I needed to get the smoke into my lungs and hold it, if I wanted to get high.

I did. I did want to get high, so I followed their advice.

I took a couple of long draws from the power hitter, getting the smoke deep down into my lungs and then I coughed. The smoke was harsh and burned my throat, but I was persistent and got used to it quickly.

Before long, I was taking great lungfuls of smoke and holding it for ages.

And then it happened,

I was high.

For. The. Very. First. Time.

Wow!

Wow!

WOW!

It was as if for the first time in my life, I actually felt normal. I felt complete. I felt like I had found the one thing that my life was missing. All of my existential angst and creeping anxiety just melted away. The world made sense, the universe made sense.

I made sense.

I knew in that moment that my life was about to get much better. I knew in that moment I had found something special, something that would help me to become the person I am today.

And I knew that I needed to have more of this wonderful substance. Lots more.

I turned to my friend and asked if he could help me get some for myself?

He said: 'Yes.'

Chapter Two
First Steps

I went home after that graduation pool party, stoned out of my head but happy and content. It was like I found the chemical my brain had been lacking my entire life. I felt complete. Yes, I know I said that already. I might even say it again.

I knew I needed more.

The very next day, I phoned my friend and asked if he could still help me get more. He said he would phone his guy and see if we could see him later that day. Result!

My friend's guy, whose name escapes me now, lived a few towns away, in a rundown apartment block. I can remember the name of the street - 'E Street'. If you like Springsteen, you will understand why I can recall this minor detail.

We drove to see him and I bought my first ever 1/2 ounce of weed.

The guy was friendly and rolled one up as soon as we got there. I didn't hesitate when my turn came and I took a couple of long draws from the joint. Within minutes I could feel myself getting high again.

It was heaven on earth.

It was, as I previously described, Mexican dirt weed. Very compressed, very dry, chock full of seeds and twigs, but it was mine.

Back then, an ounce of dirt weed cost $40, so a half was 20 bucks. It didn't look like much and I had no idea what to do with it.

We drove back to my friend's house and went up to his bedroom. My friend smoked weed in his room all the time, his parents never knew. We spent the rest of that afternoon and evening smoking, while I tried to learn how to twist up my own joints. This was my first lesson on how to handle weed.

Before long, I was able to roll a fairly convincing and smokeable joint. Go me!

Not to fulfil the stereotype too much, but I discovered a new-found appreciation of Led Zeppelin and Pink Floyd that day too. No lie. Until I started smoking weed, I was not a fan of either band. I became one quickly, and still am to this day.

That evening, when I got home, my paranoia took over. I had a bag of weed and a pack of EZ Widers, but I needed to hide it all carefully.

As I was struggling to think of a secure spot, it occurred to me that I would really enjoy one more smoke, before bed. So I rolled one up, cracked open a window, closed my bedroom door and took a big risk. Paranoia or not, I lit the joint. The need for weed outweighed my fear of discovery.

I took deep drags off the little single skinner I rolled, and held it in my lungs as long as I could, before blowing it out the open window as hard as I could. I smoked the entire thing all the way down to the roach.

And I made a mental note that I needed to get a roach clip. And a pipe. And a bong. And more rolling papers. You need a lot of accoutrements and accessories, if you're going to be 'on drugs'.

I got high in my room for the very first time, but certainly not the last. I moved out around a year later, but regularly toked in my bedroom in my parents' house every day after that. I got away with it. Of course I did. It wasn't difficult to do this behind my parents back.

And from that point on, I was a regular, daily smoker, as I still am, to this day, some 35 years later.

I saw that first dealer nearly weekly for months, before he disappeared. He was always reliable and well-stocked until one day, I phoned him and without warning the line was disconnected.

My friend, who introduced me to the dealer, had enlisted and become a Marine, so I had no other way to track the dealer down. This was a very disruptive and disturbing development. The only guy I knew who sold weed had dropped off the face of the planet, with no way to find him,

I needed another, new source, and soon.

And thus my life long quest to insure a continuous supply of cannabis began in earnest. And it's a hunt that never, ever ends.

Chapter Three
Indica

So there I was, with a new found love of cannabis and no one to sell me any.

Sound familiar? We all go through dry spells, but this was my first. And it wouldn't be my last.

I asked a guy I worked with at the time, who was a smoker, if he knew anyone helpful. It turned out he did. The new guy lived a bit further away from me, but he stocked a much better product.

The new guy, whose name I also can't remember, had a variety of weed available. He had commercial Mexican dirt weed, he had chocolate Thai, but he also had something better, that he called 'Indica'.

The 'Indica' came in three grades. If you are a smoker today, you would recognise the well-manicured, tight, baby fist sized buds that were the 'A' grade, but back in 1982 this was a revelation to me.

He said the Indica was grown hydroponically on an indoor farm, somewhere in New York City. It was seedless, practically twig-less, very sticky and absolutely glistening with trichomes. The crystal encrusted buds sparkled when the light hit them.

It also had a smell that was unlikely any other weed I'd had before. Strong, sweet and pungent at the same time, you would be overcome by it as soon as you opened up the bag.

I can't recall the price, but it was significantly more expensive than dirt weed and definitely worth it. When smoked, the taste was very distinctive, and like the odour, sweet and pungent at the same time.

And the head was, well, it was unlike anything I had ever had before. There was an intensity and a purity to it that would make me a lifelong fan.

Even back then, in 1982, we called it something that has become synonymous with strong weed. Because of the strong odour and taste, we called it 'skunk'.

Now, here in the future, we know that skunk (technically Super Skunk) is one strain of many, but in the UK, it has become something of a derogatory tabloid term for domestically grown weed. Its usage, while very common, is factually incorrect, but when did that ever stop the newspapers from printing something?

'Skunk', as the tabloids use the term, means weed grown domestically indoors, with high THC levels and very low CBD levels. It's not grown to be good, it's grown to be profitable. It comes out badly because the crops are turned around quickly and not flushed or finished properly. It's not dried or cured well either. UK domestic weed is not very good, but it's mostly all you can find these days in real life.

Legal weed in the US and Canada is grown and cured properly and a much better smoke, if you can source it outside North America. You've also got a much wider range of strains available, and it's also labelled with THC and CBD levels. Just sayin'.

So out of my 35 years of daily dope smoking, I've mostly been able to smoke very good weed for 34 of those years. It pays to have the right friends and to know the difference between good and bad weed.

This hippy is a connoisseur.

I visited this new guy regularly for a couple of years. He was reliable and always well-stocked. I was lucky.

He did stock other drugs, but I had no interest in them at this point. I do remember him offering me some pills, that he said were a new type of MDA. I now know this was MDMA, which you might know as ecstasy or Molly today. It didn't get popular until the late 80s and early 90s and I missed out on a chance to sample it long before anyone else. So it goes.

My Indica guy also had hash, and it was the first hashish I'd ever seen or taken. For all you history buffs out there, the hash he had was stamped in gold with these words: "Free Afghanistan Now". The Mujahideen were exporting it to raise money to fight the Soviet occupation at the time. It's another benefit of the black market, drugs can be used to raise money for secret wars.

The Mujahideen were America's allies at the time, until they became the Taliban. The Taliban still export drugs today, hash, opium and heroin, only now they use the proceeds to fight America. Times change, the ways of raising money don't seem to ever change. Take the sale out of their hands, legalise and regulate and less money will go to bad guys. It really would be easy.

And just to clarify, while this dealer called his good weed Indica, I now know that Indica is one of the two main types of cannabis, the other being Sativa.

Indica gives you more of a body high and is known for causing couch lock. Sativa gives you an uplifting high and is often described as a good day time smoke that gives you energy. That might surprise you, that weed can give you an uplifting and energetic buzz, but that's what a good sativa dominant strain can do.

Those are very simplistic explanations and there are many people who prefer one or the other. There are even some people who say there is no difference between Indicas and Sativas. They say the terpene profile of the strain has more to do with the different effects you will get when you ingest it. Who knows? Research has been limited, mainly because of prohibition, but that is starting to change.

Skunk is blamed for all sorts of mayhem in the UK, but that reputation is as unjustified as its name. The strains you can get in the UK tend towards sativas and hybrids. Anything with 'haze' in its name, like Lemon Haze, Super Silver Haze, are all sativa dominant. Kushes, like OG Kush, or Purple Kush are Indica dominant strains.

And the UK's own, home grown strain, the legendary 'Cheese', is a clone only hybrid. The only way to grow it is to get a cutting. Any seeds labelled Cheese are not pure UK Cheese, though they may share some genetics.

I had one other dealer, right around this time and it was someone else I worked with. She and her husband were heavy dope smokers and they dealt a bit to offset the cost of their own. They would buy a quarter pound, sell three ounces and keep the fourth.

That was the dealer split. If you had a connection for weight, the cost of a quarter pound, wholesale, was the same as three ounces at the retail price. So if you punted three ounces, the fourth was one paid for and effectively free. It made sense.

Buying from this middle-class, married couple seemed very normal to me, like if you had a friend who sold Tupperware or Avon Cosmetics. He was a fireman, she worked in my office, they had three children. Visiting them was pleasant, friendly and exceptionally ordinary. There was no danger, no sketchy neighbourhoods, no scary characters. It was all very mundane, suburban and normal.

Confession time: I tried to deal, once.

I bought a quarter pound of some chocolate Thai from my Indica guy, with a view to selling off three ounces of it to pay for the one I was planning on keeping. Spoiler alert: I smoked all four ounces myself and didn't sell even a gram of it. It was an experiment that I would never attempt to repeat. I liked the stuff far too much to part with any of it and I never bought that much at one time, ever again.

Chapter Four
"ITA"

One of the problems with all the lies and misinformation about weed, is that eventually you discover the truth... that marijuana is a wonderful and beneficial substance. You then start to wonder what else the powers that be have lied about when it comes to drugs.

As it turns out, just about everything you know about drugs is probably wrong.

Don't believe me? Check out Dr. Carl Hart from Columbia University, where he is a professor of psychology and psychiatry, specialising in drug abuse and addiction. And check out his book, 'High Price'. He knows his stuff and fights all the lies with science and facts. Thanks, Doc!

Once it sunk in that everything I knew was wrong, I became more open to experimenting with other substances.

I was ITA for many, many years.

What's ITA?

I'll Take Anything!

I had a rule, if it was offered, I said yes. And please. Manners still count.

Example: In the early 80s, a friend of mine pledged a fraternity and invited me to a party at his frat house. I turned up with my long hair and a couple of rock chicks. It was a keg party and weed smoking was verboten inside the frat house. No problem, we went outside to smoke.

While outside, a couple of local guys caught a whiff and asked for some, but in return offered me some speed. 'A blow for a blow', is what one of them said.

The girls declined, but I dove in head first and snorted a rather large bump of some mystery white powder.

I started bouncing on my feet. I was full of energy and really happy. I was also suddenly sober, so I lit another joint and had some more beer. I suggested we walk to NYC, it was only about 70 miles away.

Speed is not a drug I needed, but I was glad I tried it. It was fun, but it wasn't one I would feel the need to ever take again.

Example: A friend of mine gave me a microdot of mescaline, this would have been 1982. I went to see The Police (the band with Sting, not the local constabulary) at a very large venue. We smoked a lot of weed and drank as well. I was in no condition to drive after the concert, one of my friends had to take the wheel for the long ride home.

This was my first experience with psychedelics. I knew nothing about what I was taking, but I took it anyway. Not smart, but I learned my lesson. Don't mix it with booze!

There was one drug I had no interest in trying, way back when, and that drug was Angel Dust, or PCP. It was never offered, I never found anyone trying to sell it, but there were rumours in the 80s of 'dusted weed' being sold without warning. In other words, you would buy weed and discover it was dusted with PCP, after you smoked some.

PCP is a dissociative, like Ketamine. The effects don't sound pleasant. I hated Ketamine when I tried it, so I expect I wouldn't have enjoyed Angel Dust either.

This never made sense to me, people selling secretly dusted weed. Angel Dust costs money. Why would anyone spray it on to decent weed and not charge a premium? If anyone had any, it would have cost more. People don't just give drugs away for free. It would have been a selling point.

Rumours about drugs aren't always true.

In the early 80s, while going to university, I worked in an office that was very substance friendly. Everyone I worked with drank, smoked and snorted, pretty much all the time.

Aside from the party atmosphere, it was the perfect job for me, because they allowed me to work flexible hours around my university classes. That meant I started in the late afternoon and worked until late evening.

The other people in the department started early in the morning, around 7am or 8am. Their day began in the car park, for beers and joints, before the beginning of their shifts, with lines of cocaine as pick me ups, throughout the day.

Many workplaces were just like mine, filled with 24-hour party people.

One of my colleagues lived with her boyfriend and he was the office cocaine dealer. She was incredibly beautiful, which was the norm. Coke dealers always get the hot girls. She kept the office supplied and she could arrange for you to see her boyfriend, if you were looking for more than the odd gram.

I had never done coke before, but naturally I was curious, so when it was finally offered, I did not decline.

Coke is a powerful drug. It provides euphoric self-confidence when you take it. Throw a bit of booze into the mix (a dangerous combo), and you feel like you are invincible.

I didn't become instantly addicted, not even close, but I did like the stuff and used it on and off for around 20 years. I haven't touched any since 2002, around the same time I gave up liquor. But that's another story that I will return to later.

This office had a darkroom for processing film. It was windowless, private and had a very powerful extractor fan that sucked out all the air and sent it directly outside, so it was perfect for smoking weed and snorting coke. We all spent a lot of time in there.

It was a young department. The oldest person, the supervisor, was early 30s, the rest of us were in our 20s. Our partying was well known and legendary, but we never missed a deadline and our work was always on point. As long as the work got done, no one really minded what we got up to in the dark.

The worst experience I had in this department was the day they almost killed me and the drug involved may surprise you.

It was my 19th birthday and they took me out to a bar for lunch and bought me way too many drinks. Shots, cocktails, beer, it all just kept coming. And I thought I could just head back to the office and get on with my work, and coast through the rest of the afternoon.

No such luck. Instead, they instructed me to make a delivery to one of our clients, around 70 miles away.

Yep, they all thought it was very funny to make me, the youngster, drive out to a client's office to make this delivery. I shouldn't have been driving, I shouldn't have even been walking, but I set off on my epic journey anyway.

Back in the 80s, drunk driving wasn't taken that seriously and the penalties were ridiculously light, unlike the laws today. But the risk wasn't arrest or a traffic ticket, it was: death.

I got lost, it took me ages to find the place, but I eventually got there. And by the time I was on my way back towards the office and home, I was no longer drunk. It was more of hangover at that point.

You don't need to tell me. This was stupid. I was a dumb kid. I may have mentioned that already. I should have refused to make the delivery. But I didn't know I could say no, I just did what I was told. Hardly a good excuse, but it's the only one I've got.

Don't hate me for this youthful indiscretion. Don't hate me at all. I crave your love and approval. So do that instead.

With every new drug experience, I learned something and with this overindulgence of alcohol, I learned that I should never ever, drive drunk. And after that day, I never did again.

I also learned that I liked cocaine and psychedelics, and that flirtation would continue for decades. And with the psychedelics, it continues to this day, though I don't get to do them very often any more.

I gave up being ITA nearly 14 years ago, but I continue to keep an open mind. Who knows what I might be offered, one day? I might say yes. Try me. Please.

Chapter Five
The Big Green Apple

In the mid 80s, I moved to New York City. Well, just outside of it, but near enough that my commute into the city took next to no time. I lived in the shadow of the Big Apple, close enough that I could taste it. I had transferred to New York University to study film and TV production.

Again, I was without a connection, but this time in a brand new location. I asked some of my fellow students, but most didn't smoke. Those that did bought dime bags from the army of dealers in Washington Square Park. The NYU campus surrounded the park, and I passed through it twice daily.

I don't recommend buying drugs on the street, but needs must and I didn't have a choice. It was easy enough to do, the park was lousy with dealers, whispering 'sensi, sensi' as you crossed the open spaces of the park.

The transactions were quick and painless. You would make eye contact with the first guy, tell him what you wanted, then he would nod to another guy, who would quickly come over and make the exchange. Ten dollars got you about a gram of reasonable weed. It was not as nice as the Indica I'd left behind, but it was better than Mexican dirt weed.

They called it 'sensi', which was short for sinsemilla, and was another name for decent, seedless buds. They said this type of weed was from California. Maybe it was, I had no way of knowing for sure.

Seedless weed just meant the plants were unpollinated females. Once a plant is pollinated, it goes to seed, rather than flowers. The flowers are where it's at. The flowers have the highest concentration of THC, the active ingredient in weed that gets you high.

In 1980s NYC, sensi was considered commercial weed, the same way Mexican dirt weed was often referred to as commercial weed in the suburbs.

I successfully kept myself high for a year or so this way, and then everything on the street changed. Crack cocaine arrived and nothing was the same after that.

The first time I got ripped off buying weed in Washington Square Park, I was surprised. I got home and discovered that instead of weed, I was sold some weed substitute that was available in headshops around this time. In the bag, the buds looked like the real thing, but upon closer inspection, you could tell something was wrong. The buds were firmer and harder and didn't smell anything like real weed.

Naturally, I smoked it anyway, or tried to, and it was a waste of my time and my money. And I didn't have any weed. It sucked.

The next time I went shopping in the park, I made sure to sniff the bag before paying. If it smelled right, it was a good night, if it smelled wrong, I would move along.

The dealers got wise to this and began to put a pinch of real weed on top of the 'whack weed'. That's what the fake stuff was called by the dealers. 'It's not whack weed', they would say, as they assured you it was sensi. And when you opened the bag and sniffed it, it would have the correct aroma. And then you would get home and discover you were ripped off again.

Crack cocaine was the reason. All the dealers had quickly become crackheads and ripping off poor students was the easiest way to fund their new, highly addictive habit. It effectively ruined the weed scene in Washington Square Park. And Union Square Park. And Central Park. It messed up everything on the street.

I'm not one to subscribe to drug hysteria, but with crack, you could believe the hype. The street changed, the vibe changed. People in Washington Square Park were more desperate than ever for money and they would quite happily con you out of your $10 with fake weed, because coincidently, a rock of crack cost exactly 10 bucks too.

Crack is a powerful drug, but then so is cocaine. They are both the same drug. Smoking crack might give you a slightly quicker hit, but essentially they do the same thing to your brain. The big difference? Price.

Crack was sold in ten-dollar servings, making it an affordable street price. Powdered cocaine, if memory serves, was around one-hundred bucks for a gram back then, which was also considered a serving. Even if you could find someone selling half-grams, that's still fifty bucks. That was still a lot of money.

And even though the main difference between crack and coke was financial, the crazy 80s anti-drug hysteria meant the penalties for possession of crack were much more severe than powder.

Coincidentally, people of colour tended by use crack, while all the rich white folks preferred powder. Just sayin'…

I tried crack, once. A Washington Square weed dealer invited me to sample some and as I was ITA, I said yes.

We wandered out of the park to a nearby apartment building in the West Village. The weed dealer hit all the doorbells until someone mindlessly buzzed us in. We went under the stairwell, off the main hallway on the ground floor and he got out a glass pipe.

He had a blowtorch-like lighter and he dropped a small rock into the pipe and lit it. He took a long, deep draw and held the smoke in. When it was my turn, I did the same, though he worked the fancy lighter for me.

I took a massive lungful of crack smoke and the rush was almost instant. It reminded me of snorting coke, but it was a bit more intense. I wasn't instantly addicted and it didn't leave me wanting more. The other guy took one more hit and I thanked him and we parted company.

No, I don't recommend following street-dealing strangers into someone else's apartment building to smoke crack. But it was an interesting little adventure, nonetheless. I would not smoke crack ever again.

I was still a bit stuck for weed, as the park was my only connection and everyone else I knew that smoked, scored in the park too.

A good friend of mine was on the case. He was determined to find us a better connection. So was I. One way or another, we would find a new dealer.

As a drug user, an inordinate amount of time is spent, wasted and lost, trying to find good drugs and the people who will sell them to you. Or waiting for someone to turn up with good drugs. There's always a lot of waiting. That's the game you signed up to play, when you became a recreational drug user.

There are many myths about drugs, but none as silly as the myth of the drug pusher. There are no people standing on street corners, trying to get you hooked. Even the guy who gave me that hit of crack didn't try to sell me any. He was just being nice.

Yes, I said he was just being nice. It happens.

Finding good drugs and good drug dealers is hard work. And when you do find one, hang on to them and keep them sweet, unless you want to be looking for another one.

I asked around at NYU and a girl in one of my classes knew a guy who lived way downtown, near Wall Street. She said she would take me to see him and arranged an introduction.

After class, we took the subway to this dealer's apartment. It was in a high rise block, not far from the old World Trade Centre. This would have been 1986, 15 years before those buildings crumbled live on TV. Maybe you heard about it?

The guy was a few years older than us and he worked as a stock trader on Wall Street. He mainly sold coke, which was out of my price range and not really of much interest to me at the time, but he also had weed. It was my old friend, Mexican dirt weed, only he wanted 60 bucks for an ounce, a 50% price increase from my days in the suburbs.

The guy rolled up a joint and the three of us got high. Dirt weed or not, the shit did the job.

And of course, I bought some. It was the first real weed I had seen in a while. Even though it wasn't very good, and it was more expensive than it should have been, it was still weed. Anything is better than nothing.

We left the guy's apartment and I thanked my friend and we went our separate ways. My big bag of weed was hastily shoved into the inside pocket of my denim jacket and I jumped on the subway.

I can remember standing in the middle of the carriage, holding on to the handrail, swaying with the motion of the train. A guy in a business suit was trying to catch my eye, which I thought was strange. He finally spoke to me. He said: 'You're showing.'

It took me a moment to realise what he was telling me. The bag in my inner jacket pocket was hanging out and visible to anyone who looked at me, Talk about dangerous. Talk about stupid!

I did tell you I was a dumb kid from the suburbs.

I quickly shoved the bag deep down into my pocket and got off the train at the next stop. I was beyond embarrassed. It was a foolish, schoolboy error and I was lucky one of New York's finest didn't spot it first. I would have ended up doing time and this book would have a much different tone and ending.

Back then, I really did look like a hippy. I had ridiculous, comically, long curly hair, that practically came down to my ass. I wore Levi 501 jeans, teeshirts and boots. I looked like I should be on drugs, mainly, because I was.

If you had to guess, who in your subway carriage was holding drugs, you would have picked me, even without the evidence hanging out of my pocket. Cliché much?

I learned a valuable lesson that day: Be more fucking careful!

From that point on, I was extra cautious. I never carried more than I needed, and if I was shopping, I made sure my purchase was secure and well-hidden on my person.

I've never been busted, and other than that stupid day, I've never come close. I never have very much in my possession and very rarely carry any with me, unless needed. It's rarely needed.

Sure, I've smoked in parks, I've smoked walking down the street in many cities, I've even smoked in bars and restaurants in NYC and London. I've taken some calculated risks along the way, but I've never lost sight of the fact that this simple gorgeous, intoxicating plant is foolishly and pointlessly illegal.

Around this time, I kept hearing rumours of shops selling weed over the counter. That sounded like a cool option, so I kept asking around until someone told me about a small candy store in the West Village that sold dime bags of sensi. This sounded too good to be true.

Once I had the address. I made my way to the shop. I think it was on West 9th Street. It wasn't hard at all to find, as it had a huge queue of people lined up outside. It looked completely suspect and anyone with half a brain could quickly work out what was going on in this tiny shop.

I joined the queue and surveyed my fellow shoppers. It was a broad mix of people, of all ages, colours and socio-economic backgrounds. Wall Street traders in three piece suits waited alongside hippy students just like me. It was around 5-6pm, and many people wanted to pick up a little something on their way home.

A couple of beat cops walked up the street, right past the long queue of people. If they noticed, they didn't let on and continued on their patrol.

The line moved slowly but steadily and after a long wait, I had finally reached the door. There was a minder outside, allowing one person inside, as one person exited. It was all very orderly and organised.

When my turn came, I went inside and strode up to the counter. It didn't look like a normal corner shop. There was a small display of chocolate and candy just for show, and packets of Wise Potato Chips were stapled to the walls.

The counter had glass panels in front of it, running to the ceiling, with a small cutout at counter level to conduct business. It looked like a bank teller window. I wondered if it was bullet proof.

I asked for two bags, slid a twenty-dollar bill through the glass and was handed two small baggies stuffed with green buds. It was good commercial weed and the count seemed generous compared to the conmen in Washington Square Park. When I got home, I sampled it and it was good.

I returned to the shop a few times before it closed down, but not before sharing the location with a few of my friends. None of us were surprised when it disappeared.

What was surprising, was how long it had lasted. The dealing there was blatant and well-organised. I can't believe any cop that passed by on a Friday night couldn't work out what was going on. People reckoned the police were in on the action, which was entirely possible and completely unverifiable.

That's the thing, plenty of people in authority know about the drug trade and I would venture a guess that a fair few of them are paid to look the other way

There were rumours it had simply changed location, but I never did find out for sure.

So Washington Square Park was dead, the little West Village shop was gone and I never went back to the Wall Street guy. I think the entire experience with the protruding bag put me off visiting him downtown again, but it didn't matter, because my friend made two other connections that would fundamentally change my NYC weed shopping experience and sort me out for the remainder of my time in in the big bad city.

Chapter Six
New York State of Mind

My friend had much better luck than I did in hooking up a new connection. But like any good friend, he shared his success with me.

He actually found two different connections and each one would become a part of our lives, in very different ways.

I have to be careful here, because one of these connections was someone noteworthy in their main field. She still is, though it has been around 25 years since I have been in contact with her. I just Googled her name, and she is still alive and still an artist. She is European, though has lived in NYC for decades.

I won't mention her country of origin and I won't mention her field of artistic endeavour. How's that? I'll just call her Mary, but that wasn't her real name.

Mary lived in Chelsea, just around the corner from the Chelsea Hotel, in a small apartment block. I was still attending NYU when I first met her, so it was very convenient for me to visit her place after my classes.

I'd ring first and ask if it was OK to drop by. I never had to explain why, as there was only one reason why I would want to visit.

I was always welcomed warmly, like an old friend. I would get a kiss on each cheek. She wore very heavy red lipstick and it showed.

Mary's apartment was always busy, she frequently had people staying with her from out of town, she had many friends and many people passing by for the same reason I did. I met lots of interesting, artsy people at her place and would sometimes stay for hours, drinking, smoking and talking.

Mary was extremely hospitable. I was always invited to skin one up as soon as I walked through the door, and a drink was poured not long after that. You never knew who you might meet there.

Mary turned out to be extremely reliable and almost always well-stocked. And if Mary's cupboard was bare, she would always tell me that 'mommy had to go shopping' and to phone her again later that evening, or the next day.

Mary didn't have kids, but she frequently referred to herself as 'Mommy'. I guess that made all of us her children.

Mary was quite attractive and around 20 years older than me, I guess that put her in her mid 40s when I knew her. She had a succession of jazz musician boyfriends and it was impossible to keep up with her active love life. Her art used to win awards and appeared in many magazines and newspapers.

Mary mostly had sensi, i.e. commercial weed, but occasionally she would get something slightly pricier and a bit special – what we called skunk back then. If it was an option, I always paid extra for the better weed. At some point, skunk was all she stocked and that suited me just fine.

I was a regular customer of Mary's until I left NYC in 1991. Of all the dealers I've known in my 35 years of smoking dope, she was always one of my favourites. When I told her I was moving to the UK, she was very supportive and asked me to stay in touch. I'm sorry I didn't, but that's me, out of sight and out of mind.

I wish I was the sort of person who did stay in touch with people, but I am crap at it. And I'm not on social media, in any meaningful way, so it's not like I could friend her on Facebook and catch up with her there. That's just not me.

But if I was, Mary is one of the few people from my past that I wouldn't mind seeing again. She was a good friend and she helped me broaden my narrow little view of the wider world.

Chapter Seven
A glimpse of the future

The other connection my friend made was unlike any that had come before it.

This other connection was a delivery service that was very professional, reliable and very well-stocked. This other connection was a company.

In the mid 80s, in NYC, there were a few weed delivery services around, or so I heard. You needed to be referred by an existing customer before you could get them to visit you. Luckily, my friend had a friend and was able to get on their list.

The best-known company at the time was called 'We Deliver', though some people thought it was called 'Weed Deliver'. Say them both out loud and you will discover they sound the same. That's not the one I used.

I won't mention the name of the company I did use, as I don't know if it is still going. I know it is unlikely to still be operational nearly 30 years later, but why take the risk?

This company was organised and efficient. You would ring their office and, within an hour, a delivery guy arrived at your home or office. They looked like any cycle courier you would see in NYC at the time. The riders were aspiring actors, male models and other young up and comers. The pay was outrageously high, compared to other bike riding jobs. But that's how it works: when the risks are greater, the rewards are greater.

Once you made the call, the delivery guy would be with you in less than an hour. They all carried pagers, which is about as 80s as you could get. Cellphones existed, but very few people had them and they were as big as the Manhattan telephone book back then.

The courier would turn up at your location with a satchel, filled to the brim with pre-packed, gourmet weed.

Each bag was 1/5th of an ounce, which is a weird increment to sell, when most of the world dealt with 1/8 ounces, 1/4 ounces, 1/2 ounces and full ounces. All the bags were heat-sealed, and labelled with the flags of the countries of origin or the logo of the strain. On any given day, they would have five or six types of weed and two or three types of hash.

And if you couldn't decide, no problem! You could just get the sample pack, which had a little taste of everything on the menu that day.

They had so many different strains, and the choices changed over time. They had Red Devil Thai, Chocolate Thai, Hawaiian, Cali and my favourite, something called Sierra. It was all yum!

It wasn't cheap, but then what in this world, that is of any quality, is?

They opened at noon and went until quite late into the evening. Business was always good. Because I didn't live in Manhattan, I had to shop via my friend, who had a small studio apartment off Bleeker Street in the West Village.

We were often the first punters of the day. One of our regular delivery guys was an actor and we had seen him in a couple of low-budget horror films. All of the delivery guys were polite, well-spoken and friendly and over time my friend and I got to know some of them quite well.

My friend decided he wanted to be a delivery guy for them. He already had a bicycle, so why the hell not? He spoke to one of the other couriers about it and an interview was arranged.

I won't go into too much detail about the vetting process, or the scary warning he got about treating the company well. When I say these people were organised, I mean they were organised. As in connected to organised crime.

As nice as they all seemed to be, you wouldn't want to get on their wrong side. This was an illegal, million-dollar business. People high up in the mafia food chain had to be aware of their activities and were most likely involved too.

That's the thing about illegality of drugs, supply and demand. If there's a demand, then someone will make sure there is a supply. And not everyone involved on the supply side is a boy scout. Far from it.

Alcohol prohibition created the mafia. Al Capone wouldn't have become so rich and powerful, if booze had remained legal. The black market economy and trade in liquor was a direct response to the government's ban. It didn't work then and it doesn't work now. If people want something, someone somewhere will sell it to them. That's why you probably wouldn't need to go very far to buy weed, coke or smack, even now.

My friend got the job and worked for them for a couple of years, before giving it up. The pay was very good, as were the perks and staff discounts. I was able to save a bit of money this way. I could also just let my friend know what I wanted and he would set it aside for me. It worked out very well for everyone.

When he started working for them, my friend was given a business card for a criminal lawyer and told if he was ever arrested, not to say anything to the police and just call this lawyer. They said they would have him out within hours. Thankfully, we never found out if that was true, as my friend never had any problems with the law.

I've never been to a legal American dispensary, but I would think it is similar. Well-packaged, manicured and labelled products, with a wide selection from the menu of the day of high quality, well-grown and cured perfect buds.

Legalisation will eventually bring this sort of standard to us all - and I live in hope that one day it will happen. Soon, please!

Turns out, most of their product was grown indoors and hydroponically, somewhere in the Bronx. It wasn't imported from abroad, it was simply driven downtown.

Their operation was pretty big, they had around half a dozen cycle couriers out on the streets, seven days a week. And they were always busy, my friend told me his shifts were non-stop. He visited all sorts of people, from soap opera stars to feature film actors, Wall Street brokers and politicians. And normal schlubs like me, too.

Another friend of mine told me a story about a friend of his, a broker, who got busted on the street with a joint in his mouth. The cops who caught him didn't arrest him, instead they gave him a referral card for another weed delivery service. The cops told him it was safer than playing out on the street. Those cops were right and did that guy a huge favour.

Remember, this was the mid-80s, at the height of drug war hysteria and strict and punitive Rockefeller-era drug laws in New York. Legalisation anywhere, even medically, was quite far off. It's impressive that such an organisation existed, outside the law.

And between my European artist friend and my delivery friend, I was always well stocked and well served in NYC.

And I didn't realise it at the time, but I was about to embark on another adventure that would fundamentally alter my life and existence. This is how I put 'London' into northlondonhippy.

Chapter Eight
Across the pond

In January of 1990, I made my first ever visit to London.

Ostensibly to visit a friend who was the lead singer in a band here, I came over for a weekend. And I ended up staying for six weeks. Somewhere in the middle of that time, I quit my job in NYC.

I was a TV producer back in NYC, working for a small foreign production company. I didn't really like the job, but it paid the bills and sometimes could be fun. I got to travel around America a bit and got lots of experience and made some good contacts in the industry in the year I worked for them.

My friend had been in London for a few years and had quickly become a Londoner. He had lots of friends, a nice flat and a band that was gigging around the UK.

In London, in the early 90s, weed was rare and hashish was king. Sticky black hash, that people called 'rocky', which was imported from Morocco, was prevalent. And sometimes you got Red Lebanese or red leb, as it was known.

Neither hash was particularly potent, but it was cheap and did the job. They called joints spliffs, and rolled them with tobacco.

To build a spliff, you would put tobacco into the paper (Rizlas of course) and then heat a bit of hash with a lighter and crumble it into the spliff.

It was easy to spot smokers from the burn holes in their shirts, as bits of burning hash would often fall out of the spliff and onto your chest. I got spotted countless times that way by other smokers.

I wasn't a huge fan of hash, mainly because the quality of it back then. It wasn't terribly good at all. You would hear stories of it being padded out with camel dung, or shoe polish and any number of other unpleasant ingredients.

Hashish is basically the good bits of the plant, the trichomes, collected and compressed, without the organic plant material.

For example, the sticky, gooey, black hash from Morocco was collected by hand. It was a slow process. The hash collector would take the live plant and wrap his hands around the buds and massage the sticky resin out of the bud. He would then scrape it off his hands and collect it into clumps. It would be pressed into bricks, wrapped in plastic and then exported to Europe via Spain and eventually end up in London.

Indian hashes, like Charas and Temple Ball, are also made the same way. It could take one guy a day, just to collect a few grams.

The red Lebanese hash was made by sifting the dry buds through a wire mesh, so that the crystals would collect in the bottom. Those crystals were then pressed into bricks, wrapped in plastic and shipped off.

There are a few other ways to make hash. I've used bubble bags to make ice-o-later hash myself. More on this later.

These days, hash oils, or concentrates, which are the purest, strongest forms of cannabis, are made by blasting the plants with a solvent, like butane, then purging the butane from the oil, leaving you with what's known as waxes, shatters or oils. Concentrates, also known as 'dabs' or BHO (Butane Hash Oil) are the future of cannabis, or so they tell me. Shit's good!

My friend introduced me to his dealer, who was also a friend of his, and a fellow musician. We hit it off and became friends too. I went with him a couple of times as he delivered his product by mini-cab. The drivers certainly knew what he was up to, but a paying fare is a paying fare, and no one ever complained.

I missed my good weed, there's no denying that, but I did learn to appreciate good hashish. And it seemed like everyone I met smoked it. I was really starting to like London, but I knew there was a Mecca for me in Europe. I knew I had to visit to Amsterdam.

Chapter Nine
Amster-Damn!

While weed is everywhere in the Netherlands, it's not technically legal. Instead, it is simply tolerated, with the rules put in place, unofficially. Even today, that remains the case. No one goes to jail in Holland for selling or smoking cannabis.

I booked a flight and arranged to stay in Amsterdam for a few days. I went by myself, with only one goal, to get as high as I could and stay that way until I returned to London.

Upon my arrival, I took the train from the airport to the city centre and checked into my accommodation, a small canal side tourist hotel that wasn't very expensive.

I dumped my bags and found the nearest cannabis cafe. I went straight to the dealer's counter, consulted the menu and ordered a few grams of a couple of different strains, along with some hash. I bought some rolling papers too and ordered a cappuccino.

I sat down at a table near a window and proceeded to roll up a big spliff. It was right around lunchtime and only a couple of other tourists were there, the place was fairly quiet.

As I sipped my cappuccino, I lit the joint and took a deep drag off it. As I exhaled, I sat back and surveyed my surroundings. It was midday, I was in a cafe, legally smoking a big fat spliff. I don't believe in Heaven, but if I did, this is what it would be like.

It all just seemed so normal, almost mundane. There was no grief, no aggro, no worries or concerns, just one lone hippy and lots of weed.

I fucking loved it there.

And that's how I spent most of my time in Amsterdam, smoking it, eating it and drinking it. I had cannabis bonbons, space cakes, and weed tea. I smoked weed and hash to great excess.

I also visited some museums, including the Van Gogh and the Stedelijk, which had some amazing modern art. I would return to both, over the years.

And I went to a sex museum, which is about as naff as it sounds. And after too many drinks and spliffs, stumbled into a live sex show, which was even worse than it sounds. The highlight of the show was the cigar act, where a woman smoked a cigar in a rather unique and undignified way. Don't try that at home, kids!

I had a blast in Holland, it's one of my favourite places to visit and hang out. I haven't been back in a while and thinking about it now, perhaps I am overdue for a trip there again. Or if I am lucky, Amsterdam will one day come to me, when weed is legalised in the UK.

Chapter Ten
Back and forth

I smoked the last of my weed just before boarding the train to Schipol Airport. I was high as a kite, when I checked in for my flight.

I'm sure my eyes were red, and I was unshaven. I looked like someone who had spent the last few days in every cannabis cafe in Amsterdam — mainly because that's exactly what I'd done.

When I arrived at Heathrow, looking worse for wear, I was pulled out of the queue in customs. Possession of drugs is illegal, but having them in your bloodstream is not. I wasn't worried at all.

The customs guy asked me where I was coming from, but I am sure he already knew the answer. He then asked me if I smoked weed while I was there, telling me it was OK if I did. I said yes. Why lie, when it was obvious what I was up to on my solo adventure? He then asked if I still had any with me, and I told him no.

He asked me to remove my boots, which I did. No drugs in there.

He had me empty my pockets. No drugs in there.

He searched my rucksack, slowly and deliberately. No drugs in there either.

I did tell him I didn't have anything on me. Never travel with drugs, especially if you know you can get more when you arrive at your destination.

When he finally believed that I wasn't in possession of any drugs at all, he let me go. What a waste of time, his and mine!

I kicked around London for a few more weeks, before returning to NYC to deal with my real life. Specifically, the lack of a job, since I had quit my previous employers, on whim while in London.

Not long before my London trip, I had done a couple of freelance shifts for a large news organisation. When I got back to my apartment, I discovered my answering machine (remember them?) filled with messages from this company, asking about my availability. I phoned them back straight away.

I hooked up some freelance shifts rather quickly and within a couple of months, translated that into a staff job. This company was big and had offices in London and all over the world. And the new boss had just arrived from the London HQ.

I'd just come back from London, full of enthusiasm for the city and we bonded over talking about it. I casually mentioned something about weed and the boss's ears perked up. He said he smoked and hadn't managed to find any since he had moved to New York.

This hippy could help!

We became friends, this boss and me. He was just a normal guy, only a year or so older than me. He liked a drink, he liked a smoke, and he was finding NYC a cold and unfriendly place. All cities can be that way, if you don't know anyone.

I introduced him to my friends, I helped him score, though he definitely preferred hash, which I could not easily get in NYC at that time.

He became a mentor to me, and taught me more about the news business than anyone else ever could or would. And he was instrumental in helping me out professionally, in more ways than I can count.

His name was Jeremy, he was getting married in London later that year and he invited me to attend. He also arranged for the company to pick up my airfare, as long as I spent a day visiting the company's office there.

I could do that.

That is his real name, and when I get to the end of the story, you will understand why I am using it.

Jeremy was a good friend to me, probably one of the best I ever had. I was lucky to have known him.

At Jeremy's wedding, I met a girl, a former school friend of his bride, We hit it off. We were a couple, for a couple of years. I visited her, she visited me, it was getting serious.

A job came up in my new company's London office, this was about a year after my first ever trip. Jeremy said it was mine if I wanted it.

I wanted it.

I was sent to London, initially on a two-year contract, with all my moving expenses covered and help getting a visa provided. I stepped off the plane in April 1991 with a job, a girlfriend and loads of friends in London. As moves go, this one was fairly painless.

I split up with my girlfriend about 18 months later. It wasn't a fun break-up, but then few ever are.

The job fell apart not long after that, but I was able to find something else within the same company and in London, so phew. I'd eventually leave that company to join a start-up in 1994, also in London, along with Jeremy's best friend, who I also knew.

I had a massive falling out with Jeremy's best friend and we became enemies. The last time I saw Jeremy, we had dinner after he moved back to London. This would have been in 1997. He basically said, if I was enemies with his best mate, it made it difficult for him to continue to be my friend. He told me I should bury the hatchet with his mate. I would have, if I had an actual hatchet, but no fucking way would I make it up with him. It didn't matter what had happened, what mattered, was I never forgive. Or forget.

And that was it. I didn't speak to Jeremy for years. I would think of him occasionally, and think I should get in touch, but I didn't. Until early in January of 2015, when he was weighing heavily on my mind and I decided to see if I could Google my way to a current contact for him.

I found his Twitter account and saw that he had taken early retirement from my old company a year before. His kids were all grown as well. I went back to Google and scrolled past an obituary for someone with the same name and kept scrolling.

And then I scrolled back, and in the obit the company we both worked for was mentioned. I looked more closely. It was his fucking obituary.

Jeremy had died, a few weeks before Xmas, a few weeks before I did my Google search for him. He passed away after a short illness. It was cancer, the great leveller.

Jeremy was an important person in my life. I wouldn't be sitting here in London today, if it weren't for him. I wouldn't have had a long career as a journalist, if it weren't for him. And we didn't speak for 18 years before his death. So much time wasted and lost.

I hate to break it to you, but sometimes I'm an asshole. At least I'm honest about it. That has to count for something.

We bonded initially over our shared love of hash and weed, which is how I'm justifying this chapter. But really, it explains how a dumb kid from the suburbs of America ended up working and living in London. And eventually, becoming the northlondonhippy.

Bonne chance my brother. I miss you and I'm sorry I was such an immature jerk. I owe you so much. Thank you, Jeremy.

Chapter Eleven
War Zone Weed

I haven't made much of the fact I have worked as a journalist for nearly 30 years. This book really isn't the place to reminisce about my long career, except for one reason... to write about smoking weed in weird and dangerous places.

I used to travel a fair bit, for work, to the sort of places you wouldn't get to otherwise, and my priority on all of these trips was to make sure I could get high.

Don't worry, I'm not trying to be some sort of low rent Dr. Gonzo.

The first dangerous place I ended up in was Somalia. I was there when the US Marines landed on the beach in 1992. I was shit scared, and the flight into Mogadishu didn't help.

We chartered a plane from Nairobi, which was the only way into Somalia at the time. It was a small, single-engine propeller plane normally used by khat smugglers, which meant it cost a lot to charter.

I'm not the best flyer in the world. Nothing that big and heavy is meant to go up that high. No, I'm not a fan of air travel. This flight was particularly bad. Prop planes are noisy as fuck, and they shake and rattle a lot too.

The flight was a few hours long, it was cramped as we overloaded the plane with people and equipment. I sat just behind the pilot. I could see his radar screen and mid-flight there was a large, dark blob in the middle of it. It was a massive thunderhead cloud, which we ended up flying directly through.

The plane was knocked about something fierce and I had to hold onto the armrests of my seat. It was not fun, but we made it through. I really thought I was going to die.

But I didn't die. Instead we landed at Mogadishu airport and, as soon as we were on the tarmac, we were surrounded by a hoard of gunmen, who were there to collect the 'landing fee'.

I'd quit smoking around six months before, the longest I had ever gone without tobacco since I started smoking around ten years previously. And I was on the ground for less than 30 seconds, when I asked one of my colleagues for a cigarette. And then I said, fuck it, just give me the pack.

I was in Mogadishu for around 12 hours before the Marines landed on the beach and it was very tense. The warlords were still in control and their battle wagons, called 'technicals', were still patrolling the streets. These modified pick-up trucks, with heavy machine guns mounted on them, were everywhere.

And then the Marines landed and all the fighters and their guns disappeared. The locals said they were afraid the Marines were going to confiscate their guns.

As if!

The Marines' mission, back then, was to help distribute aid, during a particularly bad famine in this war torn country. They showed no interest in getting involved with the fighting factions — that would come much later during their deployment. And I was only there for a fortnight.

We rented a big house, which had no electricity or running water. Taking a dump in a bucket is an adventure I would not recommend.

I asked one of the guys who rented us the house if he could get me some weed, He called it 'bhang' and said it wouldn't be a problem. A couple of hours later, he returned to the house with a massive brown paper bag, absolutely stuffed to the brim with east Africa's finest. And the cost, for what was easily 2-3 ounces of the stuff? Ten US dollars, a real bargain.

It was far more than I could ever smoke in the 2 weeks I was there.

The weed itself reminded me of Mexican dirt weed. It wasn't anything special, but it did the job. And it was all mine.

My boss at the time was also on the trip. I never hid my drug use from anyone, including him. He was foreign, from a wealthy country in Asia, and was the bureau chief for his company in London. When I told him I had scored some weed, he said, 'that's illegal'.

I said, 'Not here it isn't. Here there are no laws, so it is legal. Would you like to try some?'

He paused and pondered what I said. He realised I was right and said, 'Why not?'

I managed to find some Rizlas from another friend of mine who was also in town and proceeded to twist up some joints. I gave one to my boss.

He studied the joint for ages, before finally lighting it. He took a massive lungful, and then another and another. I watched as his facial muscles relaxed and his eyes narrowed. He was high.

I asked him what he thought and how he was feeling.

He said it was like being drunk, 'only not so dizzy'. He liked it.

I'm a bad influence on people. It's one of my more endearing qualities.

I barely dented that giant bag and when it was time to leave, I handed it off to the same friend who provided the Rizlas. He was there for over a month, and told me afterward that he barely dented it too, and gave it to another friend as he was leaving.

I don't know what happened to that giant bag after that, but I hope it got many journalists very high.

Somalia was a weird place and I wouldn't recommend it as a holiday destination. Black Hawk Down? Yeah, that's the same place. Al Shabaab? Yep, that's who's there now, the Al Qaeda affiliate. It's not a very safe place, even today.

It was easily one of the most dangerous places I've ever visited, and colleagues of mine were killed there, more than once. If you ever get the chance to go, don't.

Later in the 90s, the wars in the Balkans kicked off and I had two trips to Croatia and Bosnia.

The staging area, which was considered safe, was Split in Croatia, on the Dalmatian Coast and the Hotel Split was the accommodation of choice for the media.

The first time I went, we didn't really leave Croatia, except to cross a few feet into Bosnia to film pieces to camera. Why? So when my boss did his sign off, he could say, 'reporting from Bosnia, I'm…' blah blah blah, so it was truthful and accurate. But in reality, we barely left the hotel.

A colleague of mine, a well-known Canadian guy in the industry, named Mike, was also there. He was known as a hardcore piss head and partier and we became drinking buddies. I told him I was looking for some weed, and, unprompted, he handed me a big bag in the bar of the hotel. He told me I could hang on to it for him.

It was like asking your family dog to guard the fresh meat.

I liberally dipped into his big bag of weed for a few days, before he asked for it back. When he saw how much I depleted it, he said I might as well roll up what was left and split it between us. I was down with that.

We were in the hotel room his company was using for an office and we were having a spontaneous party. Lots of other journalists were there, and many came and went throughout the night.

I sat at a table, rolling joints, while the drinking and debauchery went on around me. Many people asked for a smoke and I was happy to oblige. I probably twisted up fifty joints or more while sitting there,

Mike ordered a shitload of room service food, probably enough for 10-15 people, then he grabbed his half of the joints and fucked off for the night. When the food came, no one would sign for it, for fear of having a couple hundred dollars' worth of Croatian delicacies end up on their room bill.

That was a fun trip, as we didn't do that much work or end up anywhere particularly dangerous. The worst thing I saw happen was when a drunken cameraman from another company threw someone else's cellphone into the swimming pool.

The Dalmatian Coast is a beautiful part of the world, just across the Adriatic Sea from Italy, and the local cuisine is heavily influenced by that. So the food was good. And they had lobster too, and it was cheap. What's not to love?

A couple of years later, I ended up back in Split, while working for another company, the start-up I joined in the mid 90s. I was responsible for taking a satellite dish into Tuzla in Bosnia for the arrival of the first NATO peacekeepers in December 1995.

My journey started in Holland, where I was linking up with the satellite dish and the engineers, who were coming from a Dutch company in Hilversum. We drove all the way to Tuzla, it took a couple of days.

When we reached Split, we decided to spend a couple of days there, because heavy snow had made the roads through Bosnia somewhat treacherous. This was a bonus, because it meant I had a little time to do some shopping.

I asked one of our fixers in Split if he could get me some weed. He laughed and said that he had been sorting people out on their way to Tuzla and Sarajevo and it wouldn't be a problem. Did I prefer weed or hash, he asked?

I replied, 'Why not both?' He laughed again.

When he returned the next morning, he had a giant lump of rocky black hash for me and some of Herzegovina's finest bud. Again, it was cheap and again it was far more than I would ever polish off during my two weeks in the country.

There are worse problems to have than too much weed.

Wait, did I just say I had too much weed? Trust me, my dear reader, there is actually no such thing as too much. Usually, there is never enough, but equally there is always more.

We packed up and made the drive to Tuzla. One of my colleagues, who was already there, had rented a space in a restaurant, right across the street from the entrance to the Tuzla airport. That was called the dish house.

He had also arranged for accommodation, in another house nearby, which we called the sleep house.

We arrived, rigged up the dish and were open for business.

Only one problem, the NATO troops couldn't land. Or rather, more accurately, the first plane that carried the radar equipment needed to open the airport to military traffic couldn't land, because of continuous fog and snow. Until that first plane landed, none of the planes carrying troops could land.

Hurry up and wait, it's a common expression in my business. You're always rushing to get somewhere in a hurry, only to arrive and wait for some thing or another to happen.

And what do journalists do when they have to wait? Drink, take drugs and shag, if possible.

My friend Mike was already there, only now we were working together for the same company. He was pleased to see me, because he knew I would have all the good drugs. We went off and got very high.

Mike was hardcore. Breakfast for him, on this trip, was usually a full bottle or two of red wine and a few spliffs. I didn't start drinking that early, but I definitely liked to wake and bake.

Still do.

Eventually, the planes all landed, and we got the shot. This was a few days before Xmas.

The satellite dish part of the operation was winding down, but the news gathering was to continue, with Mike in charge. My company told me they wanted me to pull out, but I begged to stay.

The idea of returning to London on Xmas Eve to an empty cold flat, devoid of food or anything else, didn't really appeal to me, but I was overruled and ordered back to London.

I gave Mike all the weed and hash and said goodbye. It was the last time I would see him. We spoke on the phone every once in a while after that, but that was it.

As you've probably worked out, if someone has a real name in this tale, they don't come to a good end. I heard that Mike died a year or so ago. I don't know how, I don't know what got him. But I was sad to learn of his passing. He wasn't that old and he was one of the coolest people I'd ever worked with in my entire, long and undistinguished career.

I had another trip to a weird part of Africa, Sierra Leone. It's one of the poorest countries in the world and it was in the news a lot in 2015 because of Ebola.

Sierra Leone is a beautiful country, despite its poverty, with gorgeous sandy beaches and lots of Italian architecture from the colonial days. All the big hotels, while somewhat in disrepair, were full of Italian marble. It would be a great vacation spot, if it weren't for all the warlords, poverty and Ebola.

The international airport in Sierra Leone is in a place called Lungi, which is a landlocked (by mountains) peninsula not terribly far from Freetown, the capital. To get to Freetown, you could take a ferry and then drive, which took many hours, or you could fly on a helicopter, which took 15 minutes. Getting between the two places was a pain the ass.

When I landed at the airport, I made my way to the helicopter. When I got there, a nice young man took my money and helped me carry my bags out to the chopper. I thought he worked with the helicopter company, but he didn't, His name was Sammy and I would definitely see him again.

My trip was actually to cover a civil war in neighbouring Liberia and the plan was for me and my South African cameraman to travel to Liberia from Freetown, but for a variety of silly logistical reasons I had to stay behind in Lungi. Why? To catch tapes sent from Liberia by the cameraman and send them onwards to our office in London.

Yep, that was my job for nearly a month. I would wake up in the airport hotel (a shithole), have breakfast and a spliff, then wander over to the airport to see if any tapes had arrived for me from Liberia. If one did, I would walk it from the US military helicopter it arrived on, the distance of about 50 yards to the commercial hanger, where I would arrange for it to be shipped to London.

Most days, there was no tape, which meant I had the day to myself. There was a producer from a rival firm doing the exact same thing and we struck up a friendship, enjoying our meals together and walking to the airport together. We were tape-shipping buddies.

Before my cameraman left, I told him I needed to score some weed and he phoned a local fixer he knew and arranged for him to meet us at our hotel. I remember the fixer's name, but won't mention it, just in case he still works with the media in Sierra Leone. Discretion counts.

This fixer, I'll call him Mr. B, was well-connected locally and said he could get as much ganja as I wanted. I gave him my standard US$10 for war zone weed and he drove us onto the grounds of the international airport. On the grounds was a small concrete hut, which Mr. B entered. He came out five minutes later with a big bag of weed for me. It was West African dirt weed, again nothing special, but it did the job.

You can of course speculate, as I did, that the concrete hut at the airport was a smuggling operation. Whether the weed was sent to Europe, or to other African countries, I couldn't really say. But the proximity to so many scheduled flights does make you think.

I shared it with my rival colleague, who quickly became a mate. We had our meals together, drank together, swapped books back and forth and explored Lungi as best we could.

The entire economy of Lungi was based around the airport. One of the things I learned is that when an international flight landed, there was a trade in discarded magazines. You could get the latest issues of Time and Newsweek within an hour of the jets landing.

There was no rubbish in Lungi, everything got recycled. There were open sewers running along the roads though, that part wasn't so nice.

I've actually got lots of stories about my stay in Sierra Leone, which dragged on for around a month. I am saving them for another day and another book. But I will tell you about Bob Marley Day. Or really, Bob Marley Night.

In Sierra Leone, they mark the anniversary of Bob Marley's death with Rastafarian celebrations. It's the 11th of May. And no, I didn't remember the date, but Google did.

Google knows everything.

My rival colleague and I heard much talk about Bob Marley Night and we decided we wanted to go.

Sammy, the guy from the airport, latched on to me. He was totally a conman and scammer but he said he could facilitate an invite to a big party. Sammy said would arrange a car and driver and collect us from the hotel that evening. It wasn't like we had options, but going in, I knew the guy was a bit dodgy.

Lungi in 1996 was just a small rural village, with an airport and a hotel built near it. The reason the airport wasn't on the mainland had something to do with corruption, according to the locals, and it really did keep the local economy moving.

And the hotel? Its main purpose was to house people when flights were delayed or cancelled. It wasn't meant to be long-term accommodation for anyone.

My room had its own hot water heater, but if you had a shower while it was switched on, you got an electric shock from the taps in the bath. If you didn't turn it on, you got cold water. It was a tough decision, but I opted for hot water and electric shocks. Zap!

My friend and I were pretty much the only white faces in the village and everyone knew we were 'the journalists'. Wherever we went, we were watched and that was especially true on Bob Marley Night.

Sammy arrived at the appointed time, in an old Mercedes taxi. Inside was the driver and a young woman, who was introduced to us as Sammy's sister. She insisted on sitting between me and my colleague in the back seat.

When I got in the car, she 'accidentally' grabbed my crotch, she had a handful of my balls. Oooops. She accidentally grabbed my colleague's crotch too. Oh dear.

We made the short drive to the party location and Sammy led the way. People were murmuring that 'the journalists' were here and we were given a prime table at the venue.

The venue was an outside space on a clifftop, set up just for the celebrations. A giant sound system was brought over from Freetown, blasting out the Wailers. Many cans of Red Stripe were on ice and lights were strung up on poles. It was actually quite atmospheric and chilled.

I had pre-rolled loads of joints and started lighting them and passing them round. Sammy's sister asked my colleague to come to the bar with her and they disappeared together. While they were away, Sammy asked me if I liked his sister. He told me I could have her for the night, if I wanted.

When I thanked him for his kind offer and declined, he told me I was weak and not a man and afraid to sleep with an African woman. He asked me if I was married, I said yes (I wasn't). He replied that if my wife wasn't in Sierra Leone, then I wasn't married, so what was the problem?

You can't fault his logic or his persistence.

When my colleague returned, he told me what happened when he went off with the Sammy's sister. He said she took him into the brush and said she had to 'ease herself' and that my friend could watch her pee, if he wanted. He really was married and definitely didn't want to watch.

At the end of the night, the Mercedes taxi was waiting for us and we all piled in. When we got to the hotel, I was prepared for the Sammy's next play, his end game. He and his sister wanted to come inside for a drink in the hotel.

I went to settle up with the taxi driver and when I paid him, I insisted I give him extra so he could drive Sammy and his sister home too. Sammy didn't expect my 'generosity' and it threw him off his game quite a bit.

He then asked me to pay him for his time that night. I put on my best wounded expression and said to him that I was very hurt. I thought he was my friend and my guest for the evening, I paid for all the drinks, he smoked my weed and I was picking up the tab for the taxi that would take him home. I said where I come from, you don't pay people to be your friends, you repay kindness with kindness. And why did he have to ruin what was an otherwise pleasant evening?

He didn't know how to respond, but realised he wasn't going to get a penny from me. When he shook my hand and said goodnight, it was an admission of defeat.

As they drove off into the night, my friend turned to me and said 'you know, I don't think she's really his sister'.

I laughed. 'No shit', I said.

I get that Sierra Leone is dirt poor and people do what they need to do, just to get by, but Sammy took it to a different level. The next day, one of the cleaners at the hotel stopped me. He said he saw me the previous night with a very bad man. He told me he was dangerous and I should be careful. He didn't need to tell me twice, as I'd already worked it out for myself. We didn't see Sammy again after that.

My last ever work trip, when I finally decided to give up spending so much time away from home, was to Holland. OK, it's not a war zone, not even close, but I suppose it was a fitting way to wrap up my life on the road.

I was covering a pre-trial hearing for the Lockerbie bombing suspects, I think it would have been 1998 or 1999.

I met up with a cameraman and another producer for a couple of days spent hanging around in the carpark of the International Court of Justice. We didn't have access to the actual proceedings, just the carpark. News is often like that. We did have a feed of the hearing, so we could see and hear what was happening, on a TV monitor. But we could have done that from the office back in London. Sigh.

After a long day of standing around in the rain, and looking for places to piss, we finished our work and decided to avail ourselves of the The Hague's hospitality. We had a fine Indonesia Rijsttafel (rice table) meal, which consisted of a wide variety of tasty dishes. The three of us stuffed ourselves silly.

The cameraman, who was based in Berlin, claimed to be a big time dope smoker. He made it sound like he was Mr. Weed. It made sense, Berlin is a hip, cool city with a reputation for partying. The other producer had never touched weed or any other drugs, ever.

We decided to visit a cannabis coffeeshop and found a busy one in the city centre. It was in a basement, I can't remember the name of it now.

We staked a claim on a table and I went up to the dealer's counter to get some weed. The cameraman suggested I get some White Widow, a particularly potent hybrid strain that is very popular.

I got a couple of grams of fat buds and returned to the table. The cameraman and I each rolled up a joint and we lit them. The other producer decided to try some, but only managed to mouth smoke a bit. He didn't really get any into his lungs. He didn't get high.

The cameraman and I didn't have that problem and we both took giant lungfuls of the sweet, sweet smoke. Before long, we were both buzzed. Well, I was pleasantly high, but the cameraman started having a whitey.

A whitey is when you smoke too much, you go a bit pale and you become somewhat overwhelmed by the intensity of the high. I've yet to ever have this happen to me, but I do have quite a tolerance. I thought the cameraman would also have a high tolerance too. I was wrong.

The cameraman was finding it all a bit too much and asked if we could go outside for some air. Of course we could.

Once outside, the cameraman felt a little better, but decided to call it a night. The other producer and I agreed and the three of us returned to our hotel. It was a very abbreviated visit to the coffeeshop, but welcome nonetheless. Once back at the hotel, I had another spliff and went to bed.

I haven't been to Holland since. It was very much an anti-climax for my years on the road. At least I was in one of my favourite countries. And I had some excellent Dutch weed. All in all, not a bad little trip.

Chapter Twelve
The garden of earthly delights

The quest for good weed is never-ending. Sure, I'll smoke dirt weed, if that's all there is, but once you've tasted quality bud, that's all you will ever want.

I had a couple of friends who thought the same way and we decided to pool our resources and attempt to grow some ourselves. This was 1992, so grow shops and even the internet didn't exist yet. We became outliers for the future.

One of my friends had a room in a shared flat that he wasn't using, because he mostly stayed with his girlfriend, so we had a space. Specifically, he had a big cupboard in this room that would be perfect for our purposes.

My friend picked up a book on growing and some seeds in Amsterdam and we did a bit of research.

We bought some pots, some soil and plant food and some fluorescent strip lights from Homebase. And we started on our first crop.

I had a job, so I provided funding, one friend provided the space, seeds and the book and the third provided his time.

The strain we chose was called Super Skunk and it remains one of my favourites, even today.

We germinated the seeds and set up the lights and pots. In a short time, we had little tiny plants. We nurtured them, pruned them, trained them. And we killed off all the males, before they could pollinate the females.

When the plants reached the correct age and size, we put them into flowering mode. How? Simple, twelve hours of light and 12 hours of darkness.

There were many things we didn't know about, like odour control and ventilation, and heat dissipation. But we surprised ourselves as the plants matured and the buds began to flower.

It got to the point that the smell coming off the plants was immensely strong. When we'd visit the garden, we picked up the scent 50 yards away from the flat. If you think weed smells strong when you smoke it, you have no idea how intense the aroma is when it is coming off of living, breathing plants.

We knew we were approaching harvest time, but our hands were forced by one of my friend's flatmates, who started banging on the door, demanding we give him some weed. We grabbed some bin bags, quickly cut down the plants and put it all outside the window to be collected on our way out.

We brought it all to my flat and proceeded to trim the buds from the stalks and we dried it out in my airing cupboard. We ended up with a few ounces each of some surprisingly well-grown and potent Super Skunk. The result was beyond our wildest dreams.

Along the way, we gave people some cuttings and they flourished as well. I have a friend who swears he knows someone who still grows this particular strain of Super Skunk. I would surely like to find out if this is true.

We were very lucky, the seeds we got were absolutely primo. And we were lucky we were able to make it all work, with less than ideal equipment, in less than ideal circumstances and with no real experience as gardeners.

We did a couple of crops there, before my friend had to give up the flat. I'm sure we got more than enough good bud out of it to justify the minimal costs of the kit and supplies.

These days, indoor gardens are everywhere, especially if you go by police statistics, who claim that they raid around 2,000 locations annually in the UK, I can believe it. Growing weed is not difficult, and the financial rewards outweigh the risks for many.

Decent weed sells for around £10 a gram (or more) in the UK in 2016, so an ounce is just under 300 quid. It takes the same resources to grow herbs, like parsley. Only no one would pay that much for an ounce of parsley. Cannabis is worth so much, because it is illegal. Make it legal, make it cheaper. Please make it like parsley!

A few of my friends were impressed by our success and other people I knew started growing high-quality weed. The good times were going to stay good, and get better!

Chapter Thirteen
Random Stuff

I thought I would spew out a random chapter on random stuff that doesn't really fit anywhere else.

Item: Heroin

While a freshman at college, I had a sociology professor who received his PhD by studying smack addicts in Baltimore, Marlyand. I don't remember his name, but I liked his class a lot. He was the first person I ever heard who destroyed the stereotypes and myths surrounding drug addicts.

This professor lived amongst them for a while and he got to know many addicts and their lifestyles. He talked about how prohibition caused most of the problems, not the actual drugs themselves. In the early 80s, this was not a concept that you heard much about. It was a very radical idea that helped shape my views on drugs.

He talked about doctors and lawyers, who were heroin addicts, highly functioning heroin addicts, but addicts just the same. Because they could afford to maintain their addictions, they could lead relatively normal lives and no one would ever know about their secret habits.

They used to say heroin rots your teeth. It doesn't. It's the lifestyle that does. Oral care suffers if you spend your days worrying where your next shot is coming from or how you will fund it.

One of the many interesting things this professor told us about, was how an overdose is defined. You might think it means taking too much of a given drug and being poisoned by that drug, but that's not how it works.

It might surprise you to discover that any drug-related death can be classified as an overdose, even if that's not the actual cause.

Allow me to explain:

Say you are shooting up, injecting drugs, and you're not careful and you accidentally push an air bubble into your vein. That bubble causes an aneurysm and that's what kills you. The coroner would call that an OD even though it's not.

Say you owe your dealer money and he puts rat poison into your heroin. This actually happened, my professor said. The poison kills you, not the smack, but the coroner says: OD.

And the most common one of them all, that still happens today: you die from alcohol poisoning, but you were taking drugs as well. Booze won't get the blame, the coroner will call it an OD. Technically it is an overdose, but an overdose of alcohol, not drugs. OK, alcohol is a drug, but you get what I am saying, I'm sure.

Are you sensing a theme here? Any death that has a drug component is labelled an overdose, even though technically and medically, the deaths aren't ODs. It's misrepresentation, based on demonising drugs. Why let the truth get in the way of sending the message that drugs are bad?

He said that soldiers returning from Vietnam, who were hooked on smack while deployed, were getting much purer, stronger variants of the drug in Hanoi than back in the States. He said because of the tolerances they developed overseas, domestic heroin wouldn't be strong enough to kill them.

He wasn't saying that proper ODs never happen, of course they do, but they are rarer than the media and medical examiners would lead us to believe.

And these days, with synthetic opioids like Fentanyl being exponentially stronger than regular old heroin, dying from an actual overdose has become more common. Don't you love living in the future?

This professor was a big proponent of heroin maintenance programmes and said that if you provide people with it, in a safe, monitored environment, you increase their chances of not dying. They do this in Switzerland today, among other places, with great success, so he was definitely on to something.

His views and outlook had a definite effect on me. I learned that the truth about drugs was not as simple as it was made out to be. Heroin is a dangerously addictive substance, but then so is alcohol. And tobacco. And criminalising people makes things much worse.

Baltimore was where the TV series The Wire was set, but even in the 80s it was known as a city with major drug problems. The mayor at the time, Kurt Schmoke, was one of the first politicians I'd seen to openly advocate the decriminalisation of all drugs. Again, this was the 1980s and it was considered even more out there then than it is today. Legalisation and decriminalisation are mainstream policies now. But back then, at the height of 'Just Say No', he was seen as an extreme radical. Mr. Schmoke is good guy, because he spoke the truth at a time when people didn't want to hear it.

I've never tried heroin, it's one of the few drugs I've stayed away from because it is so addictive. I have no doubt that I would enjoy it. I have had other opiates, on prescription for pain. They're the same drug, so I roughly know what it would feel like. I had them prescribed following surgery and also when I've had back trouble. I am not a fan, they constipate the fuck out of me.

That's actually a thing now, opioid constipation. I've heard reports that they even advertise laxatives on TV in America, specifically for opioid constipation. One advert aired during the Super Bowl this year, which is the most expensive advertising in the world. That's a lot of impacted bowels. Yuck.

America is in the midst of an opiate crisis. Deaths from pain meds and smack have been increasing. It starts with a prescription from your doctor for a legitimate medical need. Take them regularly for a while and you might find yourself hooked. And your doctor will stop writing scripts, but you still need your special medicine, so you go out on the street. Oxycontin, Vicodin, Percoset, they're all pretty much forms of morphine. You can get them on the street, but they are pricey. Smack is cheaper and it's the same drug. Lots of white, middle class people are getting hooked. From what I've read it's become quite a big problem there.

Interestingly, in states that have medical marijuana, there are less deaths from opiates because people use weed for pain relief. Weed is non-toxic and impossible to overdose on. And it's very good for pain relief. Try it the next time your back plays up. It works a treat for me.

Item: Whippets

No, not the weird greyhound dogs, I'm talking about nitrous oxide, laughing gas.

Back in the 80s, headshops in and around NYC sold whippets. The little canisters that were meant for making whipped cream could also get you briefly high. They were cheap and they were fun.

You would buy a small metal tube, called a cracker, which had a hole in one end and a twist-off base on the other. You would put a balloon over the end with the hole, drop an ampule of NO2 inside and then tighten the base until the canister was punctured. The gas would fill the balloon and you could then inhale the gas for a brief, light little buzz.

Whippets are relatively safe, if taken this way. The high is very short-lived, you get a bit light-headed and giddy and then it quickly wears off.

They are still popular here in the UK, or at least they were until recently. The media dubbed them 'hippy crack' and painted them as a dangerous scourge on young people. Nothing could be further from the truth, but the anti-fun brigade couldn't bear to see young people indulging in anything other than alcohol abuse and a campaign to have them banned kicked into high gear.

As I sit writing this chapter (May 2016), the British government, only this week, implemented one of the dumbest laws to ever be drafted. Called the Psychoactive Substance Bill (PSB), it pretty much banned anything that could be considered psychoactive, including nitrous oxide.

I can't stress enough just how stupid and pointless and sinister this new law is and it has been condemned by charities and drug experts, pretty much universally. Even the government's own drug advisory board, the Advisory Council on the Misuse of Drugs (ACMD), pointed out the inadequacies of this new law.

The main impetus of the law was to ban all 'legal highs', which have been very popular here in the UK. Meant to mimic all the good drugs, legal highs were widely available and cheap. They also aren't very nice. I dabbled in them years ago and was not a fan. However, this ban isn't going to make them go away, it's just going to drive them underground.

The ban will make them more dangerous, more expensive, but probably just as easy to get. They've created the illusion of doing something, many high street headshops will close, but the problems caused by these novel psychoactive substances (NPS) will continue.

They say around 100 new legal highs launch in Europe annually. That made it difficult for traditional drug laws to keep up. As they would ban one substance, the scientists would tweak a molecule and presto, a brand-new drug is born.

The Psychoactive Substance Bill creates a blanket ban on all drugs, except for alcohol, tobacco and caffeine, but it is so broadly defined that anything could be considered psychoactive. The smell of fresh bread baking could be considered psychoactive, because the odour has an effect on your brain. The same for flowers and perfume, it's a minefield of stupidity.

It's been suggested that everyone in the country should ring the police to check if something is psychoactive, No one wants to inadvertently break the law. The police know the law is dumb and unenforceable, but they are playing along too.

There is one good aspect to this silly law... it doesn't criminalise possession.

The penalties are for production and distribution carry up to a seven-year sentence, but simple possession has no sanctions or penalties. That's a good thing, but it creates a weird paradox.

I can be arrested and sent to prison for having a cannabis spliff in my pocket. Cannabis is a safe drug that's never killed anyone. But if I have a pocket full of noxious legal highs, for example synthetic cannabinoids, which can be dangerous, I would simply have the substance confiscated. It defies logic and common sense. That sums up drugs laws, they defy all reason.

If they legalised all the good drugs, like cannabis, MDMA, cocaine, magic mushrooms and LSD, to name a few, no one would be interested in legal highs. Try finding synthetic cannabis in Holland. You won't, because you can get real cannabis, which is superior in every possible way,

When will these dumb fucks ever learn?

Item: The one time I didn't buy the weed

A funny random story about quality control, or rather the lack of it. Early on in my drug-taking career, the guy who introduced me to my first dealer brought me along to another dealer's house.

This other dealer was a young woman who lived with her parents. We visited one afternoon, while the young woman was home alone. She was smoking weed in their living room and blowing the smoke into the fireplace and up the chimney.

She had some weed that apparently was on a ship that sank. And when the ship sank, the weed was soaked with diesel fuel. It looked very dark, far darker than Mexican dirt weed should be and when you smoked it, it tasted like diesel fuel. She was discounting the price because of this.

I took one drag and the shit was awful, really rank. So I passed. So did my friend. Smoking diesel fuel-infused weed didn't appeal to either one of us. This is one of the few times I didn't buy the weed.

There's no quality control on the black market. That shit was probably toxic.

Item: Ketamine

Ketamine is a horrible drug, a dissociative, which disconnects your brain. I tried it once in the late 80s. Funny story…

I was coming home in a taxi from an evening out on the town. It was late at night and I was on my own. I paid for the cab and started walking up to my front door, on a quiet street in a small city just outside NYC. As I slipped my key in the lock, I was approached by a pretty young woman.

She said that she thought people were following her and she was afraid to walk a few blocks back to her apartment. I could see a couple of figures lurking in the shadows and she seemed quite nervous. So I did what any decent guy would do in this situation, I invited her inside for a drink.

When we got inside, I poured a couple of drinks and rolled a quick joint. She said that she had been doing cocaine with her boyfriend all night and they had a massive row and decided to split up. She also said she really needed to come down from the coke. The joint and the drink would definitely help.

I put on some music and we continued to chat. One thing lead to another and we ended up making out rather intensely. This was an unexpected development, and certainly a welcome one, since I had struck out earlier in the evening. You know, with girls.

Just as things started to get hot and heavy, I heard my front door open and my roommate came in. After quick introductions, he asked if we wanted to try a brand new drug called Special K.

Remember, I was ITA, so the answer for me was a quick and easy yes. My new friend was also no stranger to drugs and she said yes too.

My roommate racked up a couple of lines of the Special K and we all had some. It hit me quickly and it wasn't all that nice.

My new friend didn't like it either and within minutes asked if I could walk her home. So much for what I thought might be happening. It was very much off the table. Stupid Special K!

We got outside and set off in the direction of her place. It was literally two streets down and two streets over, the walk should have taken less than five minutes, but instead it took 45.

We got lost. We were disoriented. We were also seeing things. Every bush was a lurking bad guy. The phone booth we passed had a bad guy in it. I think we probably walked in circles a few times too. This was an American city, the streets were laid out on a grid. You would need to be pretty fucked up to get lost on this short, straight-forward journey.

Oh lordy, were we pretty fucked up. When we finally found her apartment building, she really had enough of the nonsense, gave me a quick peck on the cheek and she went inside. At least I remembered to get her phone number, so I guess I wasn't that wasted.

It took me another 30 minutes or so to get back to my place. My paranoia and anxiety increased even more, because I was convinced I would never get home. When I did, I had another joint and went straight to bed.

I swore off Ketamine after that one experience. As drugs go, I didn't enjoy it at all.

Ketamine became popular as a club drug and I never really understood why. The last place I would want to be, with my brain all re-wired, would be in a noisy club, with thumping loud music and flashing lights. Christ, I sound like a grumpy old man.

And Ketamine is nasty. You can destroy your bladder if you use it too much, from the crystals that collect in there from prolonged use. No thanks. I like my bladder just the way it is… functional.

Oh, and the girl? I phoned her and we went to the movies together, once. Sober, we weren't a good fit. I remember the film, Jagged Edge, a thriller with Glenn Close and Jeff Bridges. I can't remember the girl's name though. It was a long time ago, around 30 years.

If I had to do it all over again, I would rather have had the sex than the ketamine. But there are no second chances and you have to live with the choices you make. She was pretty, it was my loss.

Item: Benzos

Benzodiazepines are a class of tranquillisers that used to be widely prescribed, until they realised how addictive that shit can be. The first couple of times I had them, they were on prescription. If you tell your doctor you are a nervous flyer, you can get a small prescription for them. And when I say small, I mean like two pills, one for the outward journey, and one for the return.

Valium, or diazepam, is probably the best-known benzo. Mother's little helpers, as they were called in the 60s. Cool Rolling Stones song too.

Valium is easy to get and you could order it on the internet, long before the darknet was a thing. It's good to smooth out a comedown from something like LSD or MDMA. You just need to be very aware that it is extremely habit-forming.

From what I've read, lots of people are addicted to benzos and it is easier to keep taking them rather than being weaned off. Coming off benzos is apparently horrible, and people can actually die from withdrawal. No thanks.

Benzos are relaxing, they can help you sleep too. It's not a drug I've done often, but it is one I am sure I will do again.

For some drugs, moderation is the key. Don't mess with them unless you have a reasonable amount of self-control. It may surprise you to discover that I do.

Item: LSD (Lysergic acid diethylamide)

I've only taken LSD four times. I prefer magic mushrooms if I am going to trip. That's not to say I didn't enjoy taking acid, because I did.

The first time I had LSD, a friend of mine had brought a couple of blotters back to the States, from the UK for me. Back then, in the late 80s, LSD in Britain seemed better than what was around in the States. It was cleaner, purer and more potent, or so I was told.

We had two blotters between three of us and started out with half a blotter each. LSD comes in liquid form and is dripped onto paper or cardboard, that's what a blotter is. I can't remember what the picture was on the blotters, but it usually has some sort of graphic design on it. Still does, I am reliably told.

After taking it, we waited a while. When nothing happened, we took the rest.

And then everything happened.

The come-up was sudden, but pleasant. It was like my brain was on rocket fuel, everything was a bit speedy and a bit weird.

Weird is always good.

The visuals were quite impressive, patterns in wood grain on furniture started to swirl around. Patterns everywhere liquified, my carpet appeared to be breathing. This was my first proper experience with psychedelics and I wasn't really sure what to expect.

The trip lasted for many hours, 10 or 12 I think. The conversation became disjointed, but remained pleasant and the three of us giggled quite a bit.

We looked outside and the trees we could see were phasing into different shapes. It was as groovy as it sounds.

At one point, in the middle of the night, we decided to go outside for some air. Sounds simple enough, but it probably took us 30 minutes or more to organise ourselves. Shoes are surprisingly difficult to operate while under the influence of LSD. And locating my keys was tricky, as was reassuring myself and my friends that I had my keys before we left my flat.

Once outside, we all felt a bit exposed and didn't stay out very long.

The comedown was intense, but I was left feeling refreshed and at peace, at least temporarily, with the world. The one lasting effect was unusual and beneficial. Allow me to explain…

You know how you have an internal voice in your head? You might be using it now to read these words. After taking LSD the first time, I had a second voice in my head. It wasn't competing with the normal voice in my head, it was augmenting it, complementing it. It was faster, smarter, wiser, more decisive and more esoterically attuned to the universe in all sorts of ways.

This second voice was assertive, but in a good way. It helped guide me for around six months, before it began to fade into the deeper recesses of my brain. Whatever the acid unlocked inside my head, I liked it and I still view that first experience as very positive.

The second time I took acid, it was a few years later and I was on my own, in my flat in London at the time. I don't actually remember much about it, except that I liked it. It didn't leave me with a second voice, though, and I found that somewhat disappointing.

The third time I took acid, it was with a friend and colleague of mine at the time. It was a spontaneous decision, following an evening out on the town. The rest of that evening is private and involved nudity. 'Nuff said.

The fourth time I took LSD is also the last time I took acid. I remember the date clearly, it was Saturday, 30th August 1997. You'll understand why that date stands out, shortly.

Mrs. Hippy and I hadn't been living together that long and we had been out for the evening. We had a nice meal in a restaurant and had come home in a good mood, quite relaxed and chilled. A friend had given me a couple of blotters weeks before and I thought it would be a good night to try it.

Mrs. H had never had any psychedelics before and being the good (or bad) influence that I am, I suggested we sample it. Don't blame Mrs. H, it was all my idea.

We took the blotters around 10pm and waited for the come-up. It was happy acid, a bit giggly and clean. We were both enjoying it, as we watched TV.

I had cable TV at the time, which meant we had a wide variety of channels to dip in and out of throughout the night. We were transfixed by an infomercial for Toaster Bags. They appeared to be the most ingenuous product ever produced. You could cook anything in these reusable miracles. The guy in the advert was reheating cooked pasta, making toasted sandwiches, all sorts of miraculous acts of kitchen wizardry. If I could have worked the telephone and read out my credit card number, I would have bought half a dozen. And it would have become my exclusive cooking method.

Eventually we ended up on CNN, when the news broke that Princess Diana was involved in a car crash in Paris that night. Shit.

Only a week before, I was at work, instructing freelance cameramen in France to try to get shots of Diana and Dodi Fayed together on holiday. This will come into play shortly, as you will see.

Now, Mrs H was a big fan of Princess Diana. As a young girl, Mrs. H was drawn into the coverage of Diana's fairytale wedding and nightmare marriage to Prince Charles. She was very upset by the news.

I just wanted to know if she was dead, so I called my office and spoke to the overnight news editor. He was happy to hear from me and begged me to come in and help.

As fucking if! I was in no condition to be in a newsroom, I was on heavy drugs. I giggled and explained this to my friend. You can imagine how impressed he was with me. Oooops. No, no I can't come in. Coming in would be BAD.

All I wanted to know was if she was alive or not, and as far as my friend knew, she was alive. He told me another friend and colleague of ours, who was a cameraman based in Paris, was already in the tunnel and filming. So I phoned him.

My friend in Paris was jazzed and full of adrenaline. This was a big story and he knew it. He thought I was at work, and I quickly explained my current situation. You know, on heavy drugs, tripping balls, blah blah blah. Just another Saturday night at my house.

I only had one question: Is she alive or dead? As far as he knew, she was still alive.

Finally, the news broke, and it was confirmed that Diana was dead. Mrs. H wailed and cried. She'd lost one of her childhood heroines. She was also on heavy drugs.

Now you can understand why I am so precise about the date. My last acid trip coincided with a event of historic proportions.

And then on CNN, Tom Cruise phoned in. He was talking about the paparazzi chasing him through the streets of Paris, and how dangerous it was. He said the press killed Diana.

Everyone was saying the press killed Diana. A week before, I was shouting down a phone line at someone to get pictures of her, no matter what.

I helped kill Diana, or so the television and my twisted drug-fuelled brain told me. I was part of the problem, along with anyone and everyone who ever worked in the media.

The narrative that the press killed Diana lasted longer than my LSD trip. There are people today who still say the press killed her, but I call bullshit on that.

A drunk, dangerous driver killed Diana. Or the security services, though personally, I don't buy that because I am not a conspiracy theorist. The most obvious explanation is usually correct and that explanation is a drunk driver.

The next day, I began a run of a week of nightshifts and it was easily one of the worst weeks I'd ever had professionally. My colleagues who were tasked with covering the huge outpouring of grief were spat upon and abused by members of the public, for killing Diana. I don't think I was ever busier, it really was relentless.

In my LSD hungover state, I felt guilty and I questioned whether journalism was the right career for me. Thankfully, the questioning and the hangover didn't last long and things got back to normal after the funeral, a week later.

After one of my shifts, Mrs. H and I went to Kensington Palace early in the morning to see the massive floral tribute that had been left there in her memory. Before I saw the flowers, the smell hit me. It reminded me of walking into a funeral home, only more intense. The floral scent was overwhelming, as was the absolute sea of flowers spread throughout the gardens.

I haven't had any LSD since that night, around 19 years ago. I definitely prefer psilocybin, the active ingredient in magic mushrooms. The high is far cleaner, purer and less artificial. LSD is too speedy for me, but never say never. If the right opportunity presented itself at the right time, I could be tempted to take it again.

And no, please don't send me any. I try not to take head candy from strangers any more.

Chapter Fourteen
Politely Queueing

When I moved to London in 1991, hashish was pretty much the only thing available. And it wasn't particularly good hash either. It was cheap, at least, just not particularly pure.

The two main types of hash back then were sticky black, also known as rocky, from Morocco or Red Lebanese. Everyone I knew smoked one or the other or both, depending on what you could find.

I was living in a flat in West London and I noticed some unusual activity at a flat right across the street from me. Every night, around 5-6pm, a small queue would form outside the flat. Then a guy would turn up and everyone would go inside. One by one, the people would begin to leave, as others would turn up. This would go on until around 11pm, seven nights a week. I quickly worked out what I thought was happening.

During a particularly drawn-out dry spell, I decided to approach this neighbour to see if I twigged it properly.

One night after he arrived and the initial rush had subsided, I went and nervously knocked on his door. I said, "Hi, I'm from across the street and I think there is something you can help me with…"

Eyeing me up suspiciously, he said, "Oh yeah, what's that then?"

I asked if we could go inside to speak privately and he ushered me into the flat.

The room was pretty much empty, the entire flat was empty, except for a couple of old chairs and a two-bar electric heater. He didn't live here, it was just his 'office'.

I asked if he had any hash for sale and he did. He asked how I knew and I explained that the activity at his flat was a bit hard to miss. He thought I was a Sherlock Holmes-level detective with very impressive deductive skills. Trust me, I wasn't. What was going on, was blatant and hard to miss.

He turned on the electric fire, not to warm us, but to warm the large brick of hash he had. Warming it up made it more pliable and easier to cut off the Henry he was about to sell me.

Henry? As in Henry the Eighth. Basically, a Henry is an 1/8th of an ounce, which is 3.5 grams. A double henry is a quarter, which is 7 grams. And we called ounces Kylies, as in Kylie Minogue, who is Australian, which is shortened to Oz and an oz is an ounce, or 28 grams. And half a Kylie, is a half ounce, which is 14 grams.

Get with the drug lingo! Oh, we were so cool, no one would ever work out the real meanings.

So I bought my Henry of hash from my neighbour and all was right with the world again. Except, his hash was not particularly good. Still, it got me high and isn't that what really matters most?

I bought from him a few more times, but I can't say his stock ever improved.

A good dealer is hard to find and he wasn't really a very good dealer. The only thing he had going for him was his reliability. He was there every night, like clockwork between 5-6pm. And for me, his proximity was a big bonus. But as soon as one of my regulars restocked, I didn't return.

In the late 90s and early 2000s, I worked in an office that was awash with drugs, especially cocaine. It seemed like everyone there was into it, me included. I flirted with coke on and off from the early 80s until 2002, when I gave it up completely.

There was one guy in my office, who was without a doubt, the biggest coke head I'd ever met. He was also one of my bosses and a very good friend. He's dead now too, I think cocaine killed him. He was hardcore for decades.

One Saturday night a few years ago, when he was at home with his partner and young children, he got up off his sofa and fell flat on his face. He never got up, he had had a massive, fatal heart attack.

When it came time for the autopsy, the coroner said his heart was completely shot and the only thing that would have saved him would have been a transplant. He was one of the nicest people I'd ever known and his death hit me very hard. He was only 50 years old when he died. I miss you, Uncle Owen.

Coke for me was always a social drug. It was so good, you would want to share it with your mates. And talk, and talk, and talk. It would lower your inhibitions and make you irresistible to everyone. Or so you thought.

Around my office at the time, coke was everywhere. It wasn't even an open secret about Uncle Owen. We used to joke about his permanently runny/bloody nose. And how he would seem all hungover and down, and then he would come back from the loo, reinvigorated with boundless energy.

We all knew he had a problem, we just didn't know how to address it. Owen never admitted it was a problem, just that he liked to party. I wouldn't describe him as a dealer, far from it, but the fact is that he always had tons of the stuff and if you needed some, he could help. And help me, he occasionally did. At one point, he gave me my first and only Viagra, which I did try.

Viagra = a hard on like you used to get when you were a teenager. I could have cut a diamond. I could have hammered nails with my cock. No wonder all these old guys are walking around with perma-boners.

Cocaine and Viagra don't mix. Don't try this at home, kids. I lost two friends to that particular deadly combination. I don't want to lose any more, and since you're reading this, you're my friend now too.

Hi there, friend.

Like I said, my office was awash with the stuff. On nightshifts, most of us would drink, smoke weed and snort coke.

Did I mention I work in the media?

In 2002, I had some tragic family shit going on and rather than deal with it or cope with it, I self-medicated it away. For about six months, I was a total, secret Class A maniac. Or rather, I was a maniac for Class A substances.

With all the coke around, I asked one of my friends where he was shopping and it turned out, he had a helpful dealer that was local to our office. He said he would introduce me and we arranged to meet outside the dealer's flat one night before work.

We met up outside a large council block, about a half-mile from our office. There were other people milling about on the street as well. Again, if you knew what you were looking at, you would have quickly worked out what was going on. And when the dealer arrived and parked, the people milling about swarmed and followed him into his flat.

These sorts of scenes go on everywhere. If there's a drug scene in your town or neighbourhood, chances are there is a dealer. And outside that dealer's house, there will be a queue.

This is Britain, people queue up politely for everything, including recreational drugs.

Once inside, I discovered that this dealer sold everything: weed, speed, coke and ecstasy. You might call it MDMA, or Molly, but back then, we just called it 'E'.

I was like a kid in a candy store, well if candy stores sold head candy for grown-ups. I bought a couple of grams of coke and a handful of pills. Let the party begin!

I was never really into MDMA. Back before it was classified, when it was legal, a friend of mine hand carried 1,000 pills to the UK from NYC. I had tried it back in the early 90s and yeah, it was pleasant, but it wasn't really for me. That all changed in 2002. I wanted to get properly fucked up, all the time, on whatever I could find.

And that's what I did, every day for around six months. I abused coke, cognac, and pills. Plus weed, but then I always did that. It was total escape from the horrors of my life. And it worked, until I realised that I was starting to like it all just a bit too much.

I kept my poly drug use a secret from nearly everyone. I would go to work and drink and smoke and snort, then come home and continue the party on my own, adding a pill or two into the mix. Then I would wake up, go to work and start the process again. And on my days off, I would start in the morning and go until bed time.

I did very small amounts of the cocaine, really short, thin lines. I could eek a gram out for days. For me, it wasn't the amount I used, it was the frequency. And the secrecy. My long-time, live-in partner had no idea I was Mister Party all the time.

I eventually realised I was verging on being out of control, so I decided it was time to stop. And that's what I did. I gave up drinking alcohol completely, and I swore off cocaine and pills. It was surprisingly easy, once I made up my mind.

Of course, I didn't stop smoking weed. Are you nuts? I would never do that. I will never do that. You will need to pry my last spliff out of my cold, dead hands. That is, if I am lucky enough to be high when I die.

I came clean to my partner, who really had no idea I was partying so hard. She was not happy with me, but she was glad I finally told her what was going on.

And that's still me, to this day. I haven't had any coke since 2002. And I haven't had a proper drink either. Even the smell of liquor makes me feel a bit queasy,

I have had some pills since 2002, but only a couple of years ago. I had to give them up as well. Not because of the effects of the pills, that was always glorious, but because of the bitter, depressive comedown.

Good MDMA was hard to get for a while, because the precursor chemicals had become scarce. But what do we know about drugs and the people who use and sell them? They always find a way, new sources were found, new processes were explored and a second golden age of quality MDMA is now upon us and continues to this day.

I binged on pills a couple of times during this second Golden Age and ended up nearly suicidal during the comedowns. I knew it was a chemical imbalance in my brain and was able to rationalise why I felt so shit. And I decided I couldn't really handle feeling that low, so I stopped completely.

I definitely miss it, but I don't miss the comedowns. I expect I will never take it again and that makes me sad. But not as sad as when I took it and crashed so spectacularly.

Weed is truly my one and only drug of choice. As it ever was, as it ever shall be.

Chapter Fifteen
Growing pains

I haven't been directly involved with growing cannabis since that first garden in 1992, but friends of mine have picked up the mantle and run with it.

Over the last 15 years or so, I've known various people who lovingly grew very, very good, gourmet weed. I've watched as the growing industry has expanded over the years too.

Grow shops and websites will sell you everything you need to grow perfect cannabis. The tech has matured and improved. Lights have become more efficient, they even use low power LEDs now. Odour control is a thing, carbon filters can keep those strong smells in check. And grow tents are a thing now too, all light tight and air tight. And while I don't know much about it, hydroponics have also matured and it is relatively easy to grow without the mess of soil.

I've had friends who have grown commercially and friends who have grown it just for their own personal enjoyment… and bragging rights. If you've grown some kick-ass buds, you will want to share them with your friends, so you can impress them with the high quality of your stuff.

For me, it was like Xmas for home-grown weed for a long time.

One friend of mine used to give me all his trim and air buds. I'd make cannabis infused butter, called cannabutter, I used to bake brownies and cookies with it, until I discovered how to make ice-o-lator hash with bubble bags.

Bubble bags are canvas bags with mesh bottoms sewn in and you would use them in a series, with each bag having an increasingly smaller mesh. Allow me to explain.

You would line a large bucket with the bags, starting with the smallest mesh, then increasing the size, with each subsequent bag. You would fill the bucket with ice and ice water, then add your plant material and agitate it vigorously.

The idea is the cold temperature, combined with the agitation, would break the trichomes off their stalks, and then they would settle in the bags. As you pulled each bag and drained it, these crystals would collect in the mesh at the bottom of the bag. And each bag would separate a different size particle.

You would then collect the crystals from each bag and dry them out. Each bag would yield a different grade of hash, some stronger and tastier than others.

For example, four ounces of trim and airbuds, which is around 112 grams, would yield around 7-10 grams of excellent ice-o-later hash. Trim and airbuds are a waste by-product of growing that most people throw away. I was reclaiming the good bits by doing this.

This is how it is done on an industrial scale in places where they have a mature, legal industry. There is no waste, there are just different ways of collecting or extracting the THC. And the CBD. And don't forget about those sweet, tasty terpenes. Yum.

I would split whatever I got with my friend who provided the trim and we kept this system going for a few years, before he stopped growing weed.

One old friend of mine was the first commercial grower I knew. He lived in a rented flat with a basement and had a dozen plants in there. He died a few years ago, so I am not giving away any secrets.

How did he die? He had a hot younger girlfriend, he was into cocaine and Viagra. That's not a good combination, certainly not one I would recommend.

When he didn't turn up for drinks in the pub one Sunday afternoon, a friend went by his place to see what happened to him. What happened to him is he died in his favourite chair from a massive heart attack. He was only 50 years old. It made me sad. Still does.

This friend mainly grew Northern Lights, another popular strain. He had no odour control and only gave up growing when his neighbours complained about the strong smell. His weed was damn good.

And another set of friends of mine had an even bigger grow op, which lasted for a few years. They were clever and set it up in the basement of another house, which one of them owned at the time. The basement was sealed off from the main house and the only way in was from the outside. Plausible deniability was the reason. They had good odour control as well. It was a slick, medium-sized operation that turned around rotating crops every six weeks or so. It only ended when the owner of the house had to sell and he moved abroad.

Another friend of mine had a grow room in a flat he owned, but he sold up too. That one went for years, but with spotty results. Some crops were excellent, others were mediocre, but the price was the same either way. He had to sell up as well, as his interest-only mortgage was coming due and he needed the cash. Allegedly he still dabbles in growing, but I'm not in touch with him anymore. I don't even have his current phone number.

The garden that sustained me the longest went for about seven years. It was very small, just a metre-square grow tent with four plants in it. Every three months, I bought about half the crop. The quality of this one was always excellent, the gardener in question knew what he was doing and it was consistently top notch. I would put his stuff up with the best buds you can get in any legal dispensary in the States or Canada. I was really sorry to see that one end, but end it did.

My friend didn't clone his plants, every crop was lovingly grown from seed. It meant that every three months or so, I ended up with a different flavour. I could really see how much the genetics of a plant could vary. And I understood why people took cuttings from their best plants. When you get a winner, you want to keep winning and the best way to do that is to clone and keep a mother plant going, which is never allowed to flower. That's how I would do it, if I ever grow myself again.

This was the garden that also yielded the trim and airbuds, so when it ended, so did my days of making hash and cannabutter. I miss it, especially the cannabutter.

These days, home-grown weed in the UK is a cottage industry. I see news reports every week about cops busting grow ops. And we regularly get stories about how easy it is, and how lucrative it is. Local papers even go after the grow shops, which is silly because they are not selling anything illegal.

Big commercial grow ops can be dangerous and I am not a fan. They produce substandard weed and are often staffed by foreigners being held hostage. No joke. They can be fire risks as well, with dodgy wiring that's patched directly into the grid to avoid the electricity meter. Everything about them is just plain wrong. And if weed were legal, these dodgy grow ops wouldn't have a reason to exist anymore.

A colleague of my partner was renting out her flat and one day she had a phone call from the police. They had discovered a grow op that her tenants had set up after renting the place. The entire flat was trashed, This seems to happen a lot these days too.

But here's the thing, since weed is illegal, there is a lot of money to be made from growing it. A lot of money, because demand is always high and the price is artificially inflated.

Remember, by all rights, it should cost the same as parsley. But because of prohibition, that cost is exponentially higher than it really should be. The return on a small financial stake, well, it's better than you would get from the stock market or any other traditional investment. No wonder people are doing it all over the place.

Some regional police forces have even come out and said they are not pursuing small grows or cannabis smokers, calling it a low policing priority. Our politicians are too scared to change the laws, but the police aren't afraid to take drug policy into their own hands. I applaud them for their bravery!

One of my favourite campaign groups is called LEAP - Law Enforcement Against Prohibition. They are very active in the States and their UK branch has been steadily garnering support as well.

LEAP is mainly made up of former law enforcement officers, who have seen first hand the damage caused by our silly drug laws. I hope you will support them too.

We should all be growing our own cannabis. It's inexpensive, relatively easy and you can end up with some kick-ass buds if you do it right.

And for the record, I am not currently involved with any gardens. I am tempted to do a small one at my place, but always talk myself out of it. Someday, I still hope to, but not today.

Chapter Sixteen
Online shopping

The quest for good weed is never ending. And dry spells in real life can inspire all sorts of interesting feats of discovery.

During one particularly bad dry spell in the early 2000s, I decided to investigate what the internet could do for me. More than you would expect, it turned out.

Here's an excerpt from something I wrote on my website, back in March 2004, during a brief period of unemployment. I have edited it slightly:

…That doesn't mean I haven't had any little adventures, they do occasionally happen.

A couple of weeks ago, I was desperate for some dope. My usual source was dry, which is very unusual. The problem with having one steady source is that you fall out of contact with the other people who might be able to help. That was my problem. I tried to reach a couple of other people who might have helped, but they were gone, changed their mobiles, dropped out of the business, or off the face of the planet.

Normally, that wouldn't be a problem; as in any job, someone knows someone who can help. Again, I was foiled by lack of work, so I couldn't ask a colleague, I don't have any! I tried a couple of friends, but by and large I am the only serious dope smoker I know, and the others all use the same contact I do. I was well and truly stuffed.

You might be thinking this is not such a big deal, and you would be correct. I can go without weed, but it is a lot easier to do that by choice rather than necessity. I decided to turn to the net for help.

A couple of months ago there was an article in the Guardian newspaper, saying that there were several companies selling grass and hash online, some based here in the UK, others in Holland.

I managed to track down one of the Dutch 'hash traders' mentioned in that article and I emailed him. He quickly replied with his menu, which looked as good or better than any coffeeshop I've ever visited in Amsterdam. His prices looked high, but the range of choice was impressive. Then I dug a little deeper.

I found loads of posts on bulletin boards saying he was very unreliable and seemed to use all sorts of excuses for non-delivery of goods, which were paid for already. It wasn't the solid recommendation I was hoping to find.

I couldn't manage to locate any of the UK-based companies. As they seem to work on a referral basis, they are not contactable publicly. If anyone reading this knows about any, web-based or London-based delivery companies, this hippy would love to hear from you!

As my desperation increased, so did my determination. I decided to use the member directory of a popular web portal to find some local people to ask. Risky I know, but I decided to be polite and take it slow, then ask if they could help sort me out.

I trolled the member directory for a while and found a few people online in my general vicinity. My thinking locally is that this is just the sort of area where there would be a take-away or mini-cab office selling a bit of gear. That was my goal, to find someone who could point me in the right direction.

The people I spoke to were surprisingly nice, no one told me to fuck off. They were all very sympathetic to my cause. Sometimes, the world can exceed your expectations, and that's exactly what happened with the last person I spoke to online.

He was based very nearby, his profile said he was twenty-something and was a big fan of hip-hop and Tupac Shakur. This was a good start. I sent him a message, saying hello and I think there is something you can help me with today.

He said, what's that? I explained to him that I was desperate to find some spliff. He was lol'ing his head off, but said yes, he could help. He sent me a mobile phone number, told me the guy was local and could help me right now, just don't mention how I got his number. He told me his name was 'little man'.

What did I have to lose? I phoned 'little man', who grunted and whispered and said he couldn't help me. He couldn't help with spliff, but he was good comedy value.

I went back to my new online buddy and told him 'little man' brushed me off. He gave me a second mobile number, same deal, don't say where I got it, and he told me to just ring up and ask if he could help me with some 'draw'.

That's what I did, and this time, I was rewarded with a 'yes, I got some good shit and I can help'. He said he was heading in my general direction in about an hour and could meet me somewhere to do the deal. Sounded good to me, so I said call me when you are nearby and we'll do this thing.

He then asked me how I got his number. Thinking quickly, I said I got it from Jimmy. He asked me who Jimmy was and I said, I don't know man, he says he knows you and you are the man that can help. My new friend said 'OK' and that I would hear from him in about an hour.

He phoned me as promised and I told him of a quiet spot not 20 steps from my place, that he could pull up and we could take care of business. Now, I know what you are thinking, because I was thinking it too, this could be dangerous.

I went outside to meet him. He pulled up in his car, with two of his mates and for just a split-second I was a bit nervous, but we made the exchange in seconds and off they drove.

I got inside and checked my purchase, it was exactly as described, a small, smelly bit of commercially produced skunk weed. I stuck it on my cheap little scale and it weighed up exactly as it should. I rolled a quick spliff and it was tasty and strong. Hurray for the hippy!

I still can't believe I pulled this off, but it goes to show you what a little manic energy and determination can achieve. I went from no possible chance of scoring to organising a dirty little street deal on my own corner via the internet. How fucking cool is that?

I messaged the original helpful guy when I got back inside and told him that it all went well. Turns out the guy I met is one of his best friends, and he was going to tell him how I got his number later that night. I would never have done the same if I had a local dealer friend, but I am sure glad this guy took a chance on me.

*Why not? What were the chances of the police using the net to solicit very small-time weed dealers? Police resources would be better spent doing anything else, like catching real criminals. And since cannabis has been downgraded to class C here in the UK (*NB: it was returned to Class B a few years later*), it is no longer a policing priority.*

Who did I hurt? This guy had something I wanted, we had a free exchange of goods for cash, wasn't I just doing my part for capitalism, entrepreneurial spirit, and the success of a small, local businessman?

Well, I thought it was pretty cool, it certainly beat spending the day like a zombie on the sofa.

So it could be done, it just wasn't very elegant or particularly safe or smart. But we all have done dumb things to score dope. It all worked out, so I guess the ends do justify the means.

But it still wasn't enough, I needed more.

A couple of years before, I discovered that you could legally buy actual magic mushrooms online. There was an odd loophole in the law that allowed this, as long as the shrooms were fresh and unprepared. Weird, huh? The government eventually closed this loophole in 2005, and it was a sad day indeed.

We didn't know it at the time, but this was the beginning of the legal high craze. Once people started buying drugs online, the genie was out of the bottle. So they made shrooms illegal again, no problem, there were plenty of other substances that were not prohibited at the time.

After shrooms, they sold us BZP (piperazine), which is used as a deworming medication for livestock. When taken by humans, the high was similar to MDMA. It wasn't as clean or trippy, but it was legal, cheap and fucked you up.

And when they made BZP illegal, mephedrone came next. Also quite MDMA like, it quickly caught on and became very popular.

Because of my love of shrooms, I started visiting online forums to learn more about them. And these forums and websites were a wealth of information about the online scene. I had heard about some impressive and legal pills coming out of Israel and I tracked down the supplier and placed the order.

I didn't know it at the time, but these Israeli capsules contained mephedrone.

Mephedrone, also called M-Cat or meow-meow, is easily one of the most more-ish drugs I've ever encountered. And remember, I used to take coke and MDMA.

One weekend, while my partner was away, I binged on meph for a couple of days. It was a proper binge, I would come up, I would come down and then I would come up again. I ignored the phone, I ignored everything, I was in my own little euphoric world.

Everyone who knew me or cared about me was concerned. It wasn't like me to fall off the face of the earth. But that's what I did, until I ran out of pills.

And that's why I stopped taking meow-meow. When it became readily available in the UK, I already knew it was not for me.

I tried Spice around this time as well, the cannabis substitute with JWH-18 sprayed on it. I was not impressed, it did not get me very high, even though JWH-18 is in the cannabinoid family.

Synthetic cannabinoids are no fun. Nothing beats the real thing!

But that was it, legal highs were firmly established now. People liked that they could safely shop online. People liked that they couldn't be arrested for possession of these mystery pills, powders and herbs. None of these legal highs would exist, if they just let us buy the good drugs!

After shrooms, I played around with legal highs for a couple of years. I experimented with quite a few, but none were ever as good as the drugs they were meant to replace.

And as one substance would be banned, another substance would take its place. All the scientists needed to do was tweak a molecule and hey, presto, it wasn't illegal any more.

Here's the thing about all these new legal highs... they're new, so their won't be much in the way of information or advice available on them. You were diving into the unknown, headfirst.

The best, most enjoyable one of the bunch was definitely shrooms. I have only had them a few times since 2005 when they were outlawed. I miss them a lot. I don't think I was ever as happy and well-balanced as I was when I was tripping on them regularly.

There has been some research into using magic mushrooms to help people cope with end of life anxiety and depression. I can definitely understand that, as the almost mystical effects of psilocybin always left me with a profound sense of well-being and one-ness with the universe. That's not an exaggeration. That shit was so good!

But the quest to shop online continued and I found a well-reviewed company in Canada, called Bud Mail. This was years ago, long before the darknet perfected online drug shopping.

The hardest part of using Bud Mail was paying them, as they insisted on a weird internet currency called eGold. I don't think it exists any more, but it was similar to Bitcoin, only without all the stealth, encryption and anonymity.

The first order I had from the came within about 10 days via normal post. It was a Kylie of Purple Kush and a few space bars.

The Purple Kush was some of the nicest weed I'd ever had. Canada is known for growing fantastic buds and the proof was delivered to my door. The buds were compressed for shipping, but everything about it was top notch. Great smell in the bag, excellent taste and a strong, heavy head. What's not to love?

The space bars were infused flapjacks, and half a bar was a dose. They were also very, very good.

I ordered a few more times from Bud Mail, but only received one more order, one or two other orders never turned up. The forums eventually decided that Bud Mail was selectively scamming, keeping the money and not shipping packs. I don't know if that's true. The packs could have been lost in the post, they could have been confiscated or just never sent.

The novelty wore off when I didn't receive my orders. I was quite disappointed, since their products were so very good. I didn't know it at the time, but this was a precursor for what would follow, years later, when the original Silk Road eventually launched on the darknet.

Chapter Seventeen
The Mushroom God

As I mentioned in a previous chapter, I am a big fan of magic mushrooms. They are easily the most enjoyable, fun and profoundly intense drugs I've ever taken - and I've taken nearly all of them.

The first time I had shrooms, a colleague of mine had recently returned from the West Country, where Liberty Caps, the UK's domestic magic mushrooms, grow in abundance in the wild. He had come back with a load of them and gave me a few grams. I didn't know anything about them, but munched a bunch and got the giggles. And I mean, properly got the giggles. Everything was funny.

The second time I had them, a friend had come over from Germany with a load and a few of us munched them down in a bar. Again, I got the giggles and that was about it.

During my dark period of unemployment back in 2002, I discovered that due to the aforementioned loophole in the law, you could buy fresh mushrooms legally.

I started to do some research, I found online forums dedicated to shrooms. I learned about dosage, the effects, preparing for trips and I read many trip reports on the different strains available.

You could get them online, and you could get them in Camden Market. I think at one point, the UK was consuming a million of pounds worth of my favourite funny fungus every week.

A mushroom trip lasts for many hours, so it is best if you have nothing important planned. Once you take them, the ride doesn't stop, so you need to just sit back and enjoy the show.

It's best to take them on an empty stomach, as they can give you a little nausea on the come-up. A little bit of cannabis definitely can take the edge off, but make sure you pre-roll a few joints before you start.

Once you take them, it can take 30-60 minutes for the effects to take hold. The initial effects can be energetic, it is a very uplifting drug. Your mind will start racing, your thoughts will bounce around a bit. And a little while after that, depending upon your dose, the visual and auditory effects will begin. Music starts to sound crisper and you end up getting into it more.

Visually, you start to see things. Colours become brighter and more vivid. Patterns emerge in textures too. Things pulse and breath around you.

It really was profoundly joyous and extremely enjoyable. I loved every minute I was tripping on shrooms.

Back in the early oughts, I was taking them frequently, like every 10 days to two weeks. I found out you could buy grow kits and produce them at home, so I ended up doing that too.

The grow kits were very cool and easy to use. They looked like aluminium takeaway containers, but when you removed the lid, it was filled with a substrate that had already been inoculated with magic mushroom spores. All you needed to do was add water, and keep it someplace warm and moist. I used propagator trays with heaters in them - they cost a tenner from Homebase.

After a few days, shrooms would appear and just before the veils fell off the caps, they were ripe and ready for picking.

Now here's the stupidity of the law that allowed them to be sold legally... you could only sell them in their fresh, natural state. If you prepared them in any way, dried them, chopped them, ground them up, they would become illegal. Pretty dumb, eh?

Of course I prepared them! When I was getting them fresh, the easiest way to down them was to stick them in a blender with some juice and make a nasty-tasting smoothie and chug it down. Yuck.

When I was growing them, I had quite a bit around, so I learned how to dry them out. They can be stored longer in their dry state, the fresh ones would go off after around a week or so.

Once dried, I ground them into a powder and stuffed them into gel caps. They would last quite a while this way, so storage was easy. So was dosage, because I knew exactly what each capsule contained.

I mentioned dosing earlier and the key to shrooming is in the dose. Getting it right is essential and like any drug, you start low, see how you react to it, and then gradually up the dose.

The dose for fresh shrooms is about 10x the size of dry. So if you have fresh shrooms, a good starter dose is around 10 grams, which dry would be around 1 gram. Dry shrooms lose a bit of potency, so they say to add 10%, and an equivalent dry dose to 10 grams fresh, would be 1.1 grams dry.

I worked my way up to some heroic doses, getting to around 45-50 grams of fresh shrooms. At that level, the visual effects become very pronounced and fun. It was during one of these trips that I first met my mushroom god.

I am an atheist, but damn boy, I saw god more than once on shrooms. Here's a song I wrote about the mushroom god. It's to the tune of 'O Christmas Tree':

O mushroom god
O mushroom god
The pretty things you show me

The bright colours, so vivid
I just love when you visit

O mushroom god
O mushroom god
Thank you for the gifts you give me

Look, I was on drugs, alright? Good ones!

I did blog in the midst of a shroom trip, probably more than once. Here's an entry from January 2005:

It just took me three goes to log into this fucking thing, so you better take the time to fucking read it.

I'm seriously shroomed to the gills. think of it as a little taster for Friday's fun! Remember kids, It's this Friday, we're having the big virtual online shroom fuckoff thing whatever.

Can I just say, these Colombians, which I am enjoying right now, are very visual indeed. I am seeing the oh so pretty colours in fucking three dimensions today. Thank u mushroom god for brightening up my otherwise bleak and dreary existence. Today, more than ever, I am truly grateful to u for all that u share with me.

Christ I'm fucked and god it's hard to type now.

It's Tuesday. 1300 in the afternoon. I'm a responsible adult, everything that needs doing is done. If I wanna spend some time communing with my mushroom god, who out there is going to stop me?

Christ I love shrooms!

I should be making more of this opportunity, when I'm actually shroomed and logged into the blog, but fuck it, the shrooms are too good and this damn keyboard is just too hard to work. I'm going to light a big fat spliff, relax and be very wasted.

Oh god, you just have no idea how high I am right now. If I could show you with an interpretive dance, I would do for you, if I could dance or even make sense of what it is I am typing for.........

Oh my god, this is good

See ya fuckers.

In the few years I did them regularly, I only had one bad experience and that was totally my fault. I over-dosed myself on a particularly strong strain.

About six months before the ban in 2005, I got a hold of some Copelandia Cyanescens, otherwise known as Hawaiian magic mushrooms. They are much stronger than the usual Psilocybe Cubensis (P Cubes) that were the most readily available in the UK at the time… by a factor of around three.

I did a test dose of 10 grams fresh and had a very mild trip. I should have increased it to maybe 11 or 12 grams, but instead, I doubled it to 20. Doh!

That was a big mistake. The effects of a dose that large were profound and overwhelming and I spent about four hours cowering under my duvet, repeatedly telling myself I didn't need an ambulance and that the effects would eventually pass.

When I closed my eyes, I still had visuals. Closed eye visuals (CEVs), as they are known. A colourful geometric pattern extending to infinity presented itself before me, pulsing and moving, almost marching forward in my mind's eye. It was intense.

When I finally came down, I knew it was a mistake I would never repeat. I've always been careful and cautious about my dosage, but I underestimated the strength of this strain because of my initial experience. I stayed with P Cubes pretty much exclusively after that.

I miss my funny fungus, I miss my mushroom god. I don't think I was ever happier or more mentally balanced than when I was taking shrooms regularly.

Banning them was pointless. You can still buy grow kits, and you can still buy spores. The only difference is you need to inoculate the growing medium yourself. And that would take an extra five minutes.

Drugs laws are dumb.

Chapter Eighteen
Darkness rules the day

When the Dread Pirate Roberts launched Silk Road on the darknet, the drugs scene went through a seismic shift. DPR invented a system that worked. Almost everything was anonymous, yet safe and it was all built on a reputation and review system.

Located on the darknet, sites like Silk Road could only be accessed via TOR, a special browser used for visiting these secret, hidden sites.

TOR stands for The Onion Router and it works by anonymising all web traffic through various other computers, making it next to impossible to track either the visitor or the site. You can download it now for free and visit whatever markets are currently around, since the demise of Silk Road.

I did lots of research into all of this. I learned about Bitcoin, I learned about PGP encryption. I installed the TOR browser, found the link for Silk Road and registered my account.

There's no law that says you can't visit these sites.

Fuck me! Talk about a wide and varied choice. It was like Amazon or eBay, but for drugs! If you love drugs, like I love drugs, you would have stared at your computer screen with slack-jawed awe.

Shopping on one of these markets is almost like shopping on eBay or Amazon. I say almost, because there are a couple of extra steps.

You put the product into your basket and check out. So far, so good. But from here, it's a bit trickier. You need to buy some Bitcoin, then transfer it to your wallet on the market website. When you check out, you need to have enough Bitcoin in your account to cover the transaction.

But you're not done yet. You then have to encrypt your address with the vendor's PGP (Pretty Good Privacy) key and upload it to the site. The vendor will decrypt it with their private key, then use it to print out the label for your pack. Because of the way PGP works, no one else could decrypt your address, only the vendor with the correct private key.

From there, your pack is put in the post, or given to FedEx or UPS, and before you know it, the drugs are in your letterbox.

Your Bitcoin is usually held in escrow, until you receive the package and release it. If you don't receive your order, you can initiate a dispute, which the site will arbitrate. That's how most of these markets work.

It probably sounds more complicated than it really is. Put it this way, if coke heads and smack heads can do it, then I am sure anyone could do it too.

This is a surprisingly safe and secure way to buy drugs. You don't even need to leave your house, or meet anyone sketchy. Over time, the vendors learned what works and what doesn't and the success rate for orders arriving is surprisingly high. And if you order something, you will be surprisingly high too.

Stealth is important, when using the Royal Mail or the US Postal Service for delivery. A printed label, a (fake) return address and a plain business envelope means it will blend in with the rest of your post.

Internally, the drugs are sealed in MBBs - which are Moisture Barrier Bags. They are heat-sealed and airtight. This is especially important for potent weed, which has an extremely strong and pungent odour. Multiple layers are not uncommon.

Beyond that, every vendor has different ways of hiding what's inside. For domestic orders, it's less of an issue, but for anything from abroad, internal stealth is useful. In the unlikely event that customs opened up the envelope, it should still be able to pass muster.

Postman can become dealers's couriers and they won't even know it. Countless packs, chockfull of drugs are zipping around the planet right now.

Studies have been done that confirm the potency and reliability of the drugs bought online. In general, the research says that the purity of drugs bought online exceeds what you can find in real life.

Because all of the markets have star-rating systems for the vendors, one can evaluate them and their products based on reviews from previous customers. If they don't provide an excellent service and excellent products, it will show in the reviews and no one would use them.

The system is not perfect. Sometimes orders don't turn up, but most vendors will re-ship or refund in that case. Just about everyone is polite, friendly and helpful.

That's not to say that scamming doesn't happen, because it does and it's hard, but not impossible, to predict. Even vendors with very good reputations can go rogue and perform exit scams.

Exit scams are not uncommon, but they are thankfully rare. A well-reviewed vendor will simply keep taking orders, without shipping them. Because of postal delays on international orders, it can take a week or two before people begin to realise that something's up. If you keep up on the forums, you will see people start to complain that their pack hasn't arrived. When enough people have complained, the market would suspend the vendor's account, but by then the damage is done.

The best advice I've read is not to order more than you are willing to lose. A pound of weed may be a bargain and may keep you going for years, but it's a lot to lose if it doesn't turn up. It's better to order Henrys as you go, so if you do lose one, it's not the end of the world. Some domestic vendors even sell in one-gram increments, so if someone is really worried, they can test the waters with a very small investment.

But it's not just small amounts of drugs that get shipped. From what I've read, many dealers buy in bulk, wholesale, then re-sell through the markets or in real life.

It's like B2B (business to business), but for dealers. This is actually seen as a positive, because problems and disputes are resolved online, not in person with weapons.

The original Silk Road had an excellent forum associated to it, that was also taken down when the main site was raided. It contained a veritable wealth of information on the darknet scene. I probably spent more time on the forums than the main site, hoovering up all the information. From tips on buying and selling, to detailed explanations on how to package products with great stealth, the info provided was a great resource, to researchers, consumers and vendors alike.

Like anything, there are risks, but the rewards can be worth it. Great bud from California and Canada is available, better than anything found here in the UK. And cheaper too. I'm talking dispensary level, legal, and medicinal quality. And often it is labeled properly, with the THC and CBD levels listed, the strain and genetic information too.

The fact is, there is an abundance of weed being grown in places with a legal system. If you secretly sell some out the backdoor, online, the mark-up is significantly higher than if you were selling it in a legal dispensary. So of course, some people punt it that way. That's how capitalism works!

Pure flake or fish scale cocaine? Yep, you can get that. Heroin? Would you prefer brown number 3 or China White number 4? The choice is yours. LSD, MDMA and now all the former legal highs are available for next-day delivery. Every drug you can think of, and probably more than a few you've never heard of, are all available at the click of a mouse.

After the original Silk Road went down, Silk Road 2 took its place. Eventually, SR 2 was taken down, and then that was followed by Agora. Agora was good, but the site admins ended up doing their own exit scam, pocketing millions in Bitcoin before shuttering the site. So many sites have come and gone, but others have taken their places. It seems turnover is now part of the system too, none of these sites will last, but new ones will always follow.

The markets are much more fragmented now and one site doesn't dominate. Instead there are many smaller sites and not all good vendors are on all of them. Many of the vendors from the original Silk Road are still around and can be found on these newer, smaller market sites.

The only thing that would end the darknet markets? A legal, regulated market in real life. Until that day comes, the darknet markets will continue to flourish. As long as there is a demand, someone will work out a way to meet it with a good supply.

Chapter Nineteen
The worst drugs

As a long time recreational drug user, I have experience directly or indirectly with most mind-altering substances. I can tell you, without hesitation, that the two worst drugs in the world are tobacco and alcohol.

Yes, I know they are the legal ones, that society and the government tell us are OK to take, but they really are the worst.

I started smoking and drinking as a teenager. All the adults I knew at the time used both drugs extensively. I saw them consumed regularly, so it's hardly surprising that I wanted to use them too.

Alcohol causes problems, just visit any city centre in the UK on a Friday or Saturday night. It gets messy, and violent and alcohol is the reason. Ask the cops what they think. They will tell you the same thing.

I drank as a teenager and continued drinking regularly and heavily until I was nearly 40 years old. Booze is fun, booze is social, but booze makes you do things the sober you would never consider.

Would you barf in the back of a taxi when you were sober? Would you chat shit to strangers? Would you have sex with the modestly unattractive? If it weren't for alcohol, how many of us would still have our virginity intact?

People drink themselves to death. It is not that hard to destroy your liver by overindulging. Or how about passing out, throwing up and choking on your own vomit? It's an easy way to die and it's the death of choice for many rock stars.

Alcohol is dangerously addictive and worse than heroin. It's easy to maintain a heroin addiction, you just need maintenance doses. Proper alcoholics maintenance-drink and if you've ever known one, you will know what I mean. They need something to steady their hands, when they wake up.

Years ago, I used to frequent breakfast pubs in London. The liquor laws here are a bit antiquated and only a small, select group of pubs were allowed to sell booze before lunchtime.

I used to go to a few in Smithfield Market. Ostensibly set up to cater to the meat-cutting trade, these pubs would open early for the butchers and traders at the market.

You would see a weird mix of people at these morning pubs. Besides the blood spattered butchers (at least I hope they were butchers), there were postmen and nurses, journalists and city traders. The nurses and the journos like me were drinking after nightshifts, and the butchers during their work day. But the posties and city guys were downing a few, before their work day began. These were people who needed to drink, just to feel normal.

If you need a drink at 7am, before going to the office, you probably have a drinking problem. And if you have a problem, you need help, but you need to want that help.

These people didn't want help, they just wanted to keep drinking.

Coming off booze can kill you, if you're not careful. Alcohol withdrawal is the worst. You can end up having seizures. If you're that hooked and you want to come off the drink, do it with medical supervision and ideally be an in-patient.

Please don't die. Dying is a drag.

I was nearly always a social drinker. Drinking and going out went hand in hand. It's a social lubricant, it lowers inhibitions. It can turn even the shyest soul into the life of the party.

My drinking problem lasted for six months, when I was binging on cocaine. I was drinking alone and mixing it with cocaine and MDMA. When I worked out it was a problem, I stopped, cold. I was never a full-on alcoholic, but if left unchecked, I expect I could have attained that title.

I'm not suggesting we ban booze. They tried that once in America, it didn't work out very well.

I didn't know my father's father, my paternal grandfather, neither did my dad. I did hear stories about him. He was a bootlegger during prohibition, a booze runner and he was allegedly killed on a run down from Canada. Hey ho.

We laugh now when we talk about alcohol prohibition. Bathtub gin, speakeasies, and flappers. That era has been glamourised to some extent. During prohibition, if you wanted a drink, it wasn't hard to find. If there is a demand, the supply will find a way.

It's the same with drugs today. People want them, lots of people want them, and there is money to be made by supplying them. It's capitalism as it is meant to be.

The difference, of course, is regulation. The alcohol industry is strictly controlled and regulated, the trade in recreational drugs is not.

Send a 12-year-old out to buy a bottle of vodka and more than likely, he will come back empty handed. Send that same 12-year-old out to buy some weed or crack, and he will return with a pocket full of drugs. There are no age checks for drugs, but a liquor store or off-licence will lose their licence if they get caught selling liquor to a child. And I am cool with that.

Alcohol controls are there to keep us all safer. The harms of drugs can be mitigated through regulation and education. MDMA is a relatively safe drug and when someone dies from it, it is through ignorance. They drink too much water or they don't regulate their body temperature, it's not because the drug is toxic. Unless it is toxic, because the pill contains something other than MDMA. A regulated market would prevent many mishaps and keep people safer.

The one drug I am addicted to is nicotine and it is an addiction that continues to this day.

I started smoking cigarettes properly when I was 19 years old. I started going to bars and found I needed something to do with my hands and mouth that didn't involve drinking. Smoking fit the bill perfectly.

At first, they were a prop, an affectation, a means to distract myself from drinking too much. And then I started to inhale and before I knew it, I was hooked on the nicotine.

I smoked like I meant it. When I quit, I was up to 40 cigarettes a day. That's two packs. That's a lot of smoking.

When I say I was hooked, I mean I was really hooked. I would wake up and immediately light one; I'd have one right before I went to sleep. And in-between, I would smoke nearly non-stop.

When smoking was finally banned in public, it didn't make me smoke less, but it did make me go out less. Part of my decision to stop drinking stems from this. I stopped enjoying bars and pubs when I could no longer smoke inside them. This made the decision to give up booze that much easier.

Growing up, nearly every adult I knew smoked. My father didn't smoke, but my mother did. My aunts and uncles smoked, my cousins all smoked, all of my parents' friends smoked, my teachers smoked… everyone smoked.

As a kid, I was very anti-smoking. It smelled terrible and caused all sorts of horrible health problems. I knew this from the age of five, but I still ended up a heavy smoker anyway.

My mother was a life-long smoker. She also had high blood pressure. But she continued to smoke, right up until she had a bad stroke. That should have put me off smoking too, but it didn't.

But in the end, what put me off smoking, wasn't the smell or the health risks, it was the cost. Cigarettes are now crazy expensive here in the UK, mainly thanks to punitive taxes put on by the government. Again, regulation comes through, as it finally turned this hardcore smoker into someone who is smoke-free.

But hang on, I said I was still addicted to nicotine, And that's true, but I take it in a much safer, healthier way. I use an e-cigarette now.

Technically, I vape. I am a vaper and I enjoy vapour. I made the switch over three years ago, and I am very glad I did. I don't stink of fags, my lungs are healthier and I have saved a fortune.

No joke, in three and a half years, I have saved an actual fortune. That's money I would have just burned up and stubbed out in an ashtray. I doubt I have spent a tenth as much on vaping supplies in that time.

I'm lucky, the UK has embraced electronic cigarettes and sees them as a huge breakthrough in health care and healthier living. Use has been encouraged. When I told my GP I had given up smoking in favour of the electronic version, she was pleased.

I'm pleased too. I do so little that is good for me, besides smoking weed. Vaping has probably added a decade to my lifespan.

Again, I wouldn't ban tobacco, I would continue to regulate it. Plain packaging is a good thing. Age restrictions are also beneficial. No smoking in public enclosed spaces, also good. Banning it outside completely, kinda dumb and I hope it doesn't go that far.

The smell of smoke is horrible and I used to stink of it all the time. Now, if someone lights up 100 yards away from me, I can smell it, but I would never tell anyone else not to smoke. I am not one of those self-righteous ex-smokers. That would be tedious. But if you're interested in e-cigarettes, I'm happy to sing their praises and point you in the right direction to try them yourself. Trust this hippy, if you smoke now, make the switch. You can thank me later. And you will be alive to thank me. And richer. It's all kinds of win!

Chapter Twenty
The Future

We've loosely covered the last 35 years of my twisted, drug-fuelled existence, but what does the future hold?

Good question!

Decriminalisation and legalisation will continue apace and the more it increases around the world, the harder it will be to deny the benefits. Even in backward countries, like the UK, it will be more difficult to continuing lying to people, when the evidence is so widespread.

If you look at Portugal, where they decriminalised everything years ago, every metric is positive. All drug use has decreased, especially amongst younger people, HIV infections have gone down, and drug-related deaths have been drastically reduced.

Likewise in Colorado, where legal weed has been on sale for a while now, it is seen as a huge success. No one in Colorado would support returning to prohibition.

Uruguay and Canada are in the process of legalising cannabis nationally and I applaud their efforts. These policies are sensible, evidence-based and will benefit everyone.

Drug policies in the UK are not based on evidence, but on misplaced fear and outright lies, which are perpetuated by the media. But the truth is out there, if you know where to look.

We're already behind in the legal weed industry. The UK needs to catch up or the industry will be dominated by large American companies like Privateer Holdings. They have the licence to use Bob Marley's name to brand their cannabis, and own the very useful leafly.com, which is a great resource on cannabis strains.

Privateer Holdings is already worth millions, and is likely to continue to expand and grow. We need some British investment in this fast growing sector, but that can't happen without a change to the laws.

The benefits of changing the laws are many. The savings in law enforcement, criminal courts, and prisons would all be huge. The tax revenue would also be substantial. Jobs would be created too. Legalising drugs is a huge win.

Even more importantly, it would end the criminalisation of people who don't deserve to be criminalised. In my north London ghetto, relations between the police and the local population would improve overnight, if the cops left everyone with a joint in their pockets alone.

Recently, my partner saw some police activity just outside our front door. The cops were chasing some kids, threatening to Taser them, all over a very small amount of weed. The local cops even tweeted about the encounter, claiming they were making the streets safer by confiscating a rather insignificant amount of cannabis from some teenagers.

Really? The streets are safer? Or would they be safer if the police didn't have the right to harass the local kids simply because they had a pocketful of plant matter?

Relations between the police and the local population in my neighbourhood have been bad for years. The London riots in 2011 were local to me and it feels like they could be repeated, at any time. It wouldn't take much to set them off again.

I don't have a problem with a strong police force. I have a problem with the laws. If you want to search someone because you have a genuine suspicion they are carrying weapons, then please do. But for the sweet love of god, every teenager has got a spliff in his or her pocket, don't ruin their lives by busting them for it.

As of this writing, six police forces in the UK have announced the de-prioritisation of cannabis law enforcement and have effectively decriminalised weed. Why haven't the Metropolitan Police in London followed suit? What are they waiting for?

Some police forces seem to be setting a more sensible drug policy than our central government. This is a good thing and will only help pressure Whitehall to follow suit.

A legal, taxed and regulated cannabis market would help everyone. The police would benefit, as they could re-allocate their limited resources to chasing down actual criminals. The overcrowded prisons could concentrate on jailing genuine offenders, the courts could concentrate on the same. And the government could raise additional tax, which could be spent on important things, like education, the NHS and our infrastructure.

Everyone wins, but especially cannabis smokers. I am not a criminal, and I should not be criminalised because I smoke weed. No one should. It is the pinnacle of stupidity to think the current system is working. No one should be criminalised for using any drug.

Getting high is a basic human right. Google it. Go on, I can wait.

I really hope I live long enough to see the laws change. It is a change that is long overdue.

The Liberal Democrats and the Green Party both support legalisation, but our two main parties, the Conservatives and Labour, haven't come around yet. They need to, and fast, or we risk being stuck way behind the rest of the world as the green economy expands and grows.

But what about the future of weed itself?

Concentrates. People say concentrates are the future of weed. That may be true, but they haven't really caught on in the UK, just yet. People aren't really aware of the concept here. It's known as dabbing and it is a very clean and pure way to ingest weed.

When I say concentrates, I am referring to waxes, shatters and oils, the refined extracts of herbal cannabis. Butane Hash Oil (BHO) is the proper name for it and I have seen this called the future of cannabis, more than once.

When cannabis has been distilled down to this concentrated form, you only need a tiny amount to get very high. One tiny dab, which you can inhale in one hit, is the equivalent of smoking an entire joint. It gets you higher, faster, with less effort, plus none of the plant matter gets burned, since it is taken out of the equation before you light it.

When the newspapers drone on about the potency of skunk, I laugh a little, because dabs are exponentially stronger. And I dread the day the Daily Fail discovers dabs, because the scaremongering will reach a new level of hysteria. And it will be a hysteria that is totally undeserved.

I'm not going to lie, concentrates are for experienced smokers. They are strong. Smoking a dab is like the first time you got high, every time you have one. The flavours are intensely enjoyable and the head is incredible. One tiny little dab will medicate you for hours.

There's no reason for hysteria over concentrates, any more than there should be hysteria because whiskey is stronger than beer. You would drink a pint of beer, but you wouldn't drink a pint of whiskey, would you? It's the same with cannabis. If you have a stronger product, you need less to get you where you want to go. It's simple.

The biggest danger from dabs comes not from taking them, but making them. People trying to extract THC at home, using butane, have had some accidents. Again, it's simple. If you don't have the proper lab equipment to safely do it, then don't do it! Leave it to the pros.

I would like to see the law allow for personal grows, cannabis social clubs and licensed shops that sell cannabis products. The market is already established, we just need to shift it from the black market to a legal, regulated system. I dream of this day coming.

There are also safer, better ways to ingest cannabis. I've been using vaporisers for ages. I've got a Digital Volcano, I used to have a Pinnacle Pro and recently I bought a 'Mighty' Vaporiser from Storz and Bickel, a hand-held vaporiser from the same people who make the Volcano.

If you've never used a vaporiser, you really should try one. They heat your cannabis to the point where the THC and other tasty ingredients turn to vapour, without all the plant matter burning. The high is very strong, but the health benefits are even stronger.

And when you vape weed, you don't extract all the goodness. There is still some residual THC in your ABV (already been vaped) weed and you can use this is make cannabutter. It's very cost-effective too, as you go through far less when you vaporise.

They say that when you burn cannabis, you are wasting a large percentage of it. By vaping, you are maximising the value. And that's even more true if you use the ABV for cooking.

But that's not the only way to vape cannabis, you can also get atomisers that work with eCigarette batteries, which are perfect for vaping concentrates. Stealthy, ultraportable and tasty, I think this is the ultimate future of cannabis.

Edibles are also gaining in popularity, especially in places where they have a legal market, for recreational or medical purposes. Eating weed gives you a different sort of high, far stronger and longer-lasting, but the catch is judging the dosage. They are still trying to work out the best way to regulate edibles. I'm sure they will figure it out.

Keep it simple, one chocolate bar, or brownie, or lollypop or gummy bear should be one dose, for an inexperienced user. If it is not strong enough, you can always eat more, but if it is too strong, you might not enjoy it.

I've read about small chocolate bars in Colorado having as many as 16 doses contained within, but without the necessary labelling to point that out. The New York Times columnist Maureen Dowd wrote about her bad experience with edibles. It might make you laugh, but the fact is it should not have happened and it gives edibles a bad reputation that they most certainly don't deserve.

The biggest change to drug acquisition and consumption, without a doubt, is the darknet markets. Having the ability to purchase very high-quality drugs, anonymously and safely, from around the world, has changed things for the better. And it's likely those changes will continue.

Globalisation effects everything, even consumer drug shopping and the internet makes the world a much smaller place.

The other big change is 'legal highs', also called novel psychoactive substances (NPS). I dabbled and wasn't a fan, but many people are and continue to be. The British government has followed Ireland and tried to ban everything. That's not how this works. All the ban has done is drive the trade further underground and make everything more valuable. Prices will rise and availability will always remain. So all this law has done is make a bad thing much worse.

If they just made all the good drugs legal, no one would touch legal highs. You could wipe out the NPS trade instantly, just by allowing people access to their safer, original forms. But nah, they won't do that, will they?

People have altered their consciousness for millennia. Stupid laws won't change that. Instead of trying to legislate morality, let's legislate for reality. If millions of people choose to consume certain substances, banning those substances won't stop anyone. People continued to drink during alcohol prohibition, just as people continue to get high today.

If you can beat 'em, regulate 'em. And tax 'em. And everyone would win.

It's just plain, old fashioned common sense and wouldn't the world be a better place with more common sense?

Chapter Twenty One
The northlondonhippy

Around the time of my regular shrooming adventures, back in 2003, when I wanted to sign up for some online forums, I needed a screen name.

I came up with northlondonhippy.

It made sense. I live in north London, and I am a bit of a secret, peace-loving, groovy, make-believe trippy hippy. So I joined up those three words and history was made.

OK, history wasn't made, but the name stuck.

And then during the depths of my brief period of unemployment, I decided to start a blog and I used that screen name for it. It was on blogspot, still is, though I stopped posting on that one, when I moved to my own, self-hosted website.

You can find my current site at northlondonhippy.com and maybe you already did when you bought this book.

Well done you, if you did. You are clearly a person of great intelligence and excellent taste. Thank you for your patronage. I will probably use the money I made off your purchase to buy more weed. Dank!

As I worked on building my brand (yes, I know it is wank-speak), I tried to think of ways to raise my online profile and presence.

One of my ideas was to design a bong, which I did in partnership with everyonedoesit.com and the good people from RooR.

RooR manufacture some of the finest glass bongs in the world and everyonedoesit.com is one of the best online headshops on the planet, so I was in very good company.

The 'northlondonhippy deluxe' was available exclusively via everyonedoesit (known as EDIT) and cost a fortune. Even though it was very pricey, we did manage to sell a fair few.

And if you are persistent and determined, you can still find it listed on head shop websites around on the internet. So much for exclusivity!

The bong, while a clever idea, didn't really set the world on fire and I continued to toil in relative obscurity until this day, when you bought my book and became my new best friend.

It's good to have friends.

Being the northlondonhippy isn't a job, or a vocation, it is a way of life. Really, it's more of a hobby and this book is the closest I've come to turning it into anything more than that. I don't expect it to change my life, any more than it has in the last 13 years.

My joke throughout the writing of this book is this: If I sell one million copies of this book, I will quit my job and concentrate on writing an actual novel that I've been toying with for around 20 years. How cool would that be?

I know I will never sell a million copies, but it's good to have a goal, even an unobtainable one. Like a blow job from Ariana Grande. I would certainly like one, but the chances of her mouth and my penis ever meeting are non-existent. That won't stop me from imagining it over and over, late at night, alone, in the dark.

It's the same with book sales.

I like to imagine that this book will sell. I like to imagine that people across the land will be reading it. I like to imagine that I could become the public voice of decent, upstanding, tax-paying members of society who use drugs regularly and responsibly. It's a voice that is sorely lacking in the debate around drugs.

Noel Gallagher, the talented one from the band Oasis, said this nearly 20 years ago and it's as true now as it was then. Noel said:

"As soon as people realise that the majority of people in this country take drugs, then the better off we'll all be. It's not like a scandalous sensation, or anything like that... (Taking) drugs is like getting up and having a cup of tea in the morning."

Drugs are enjoyable and that point is often left out whenever drugs are discussed.

My mother used to say that drugs scared her because she was worried about being out of control. I've never felt out of control on drugs, well, except when very drunk on alcohol.

My experiences with drugs over the last three and half decades have been overwhelmingly positive. I genuinely credit weed with my survival and success. I would have probably topped myself in my teens or twenties, if I didn't discover the benefits of daily weed consumption. My body lacks THC, I'm sure of it.

That's actually a thing now, called "chronic endocannabinoid deficiency" and I really do believe I suffer from it. Without weed, I am not really me, I am just a shell of myself, a half-empty vessel containing anxiety, depression, and a healthy dose of self-loathing.

With weed, I feel normal, I feel complete. I am the good me, the better me. I'm the me that you would have dinner with and find endlessly entertaining and maybe just a tiny bit endearing.

There has also been some research recently into using psilocybin, the active ingredient in magic mushrooms, to treat depression. I consider my use of shrooms, like my use of cannabis, medicinal. Perhaps a tiny bit spiritual too.

People self-medicate with many substances, including alcohol. I prefer weed and shrooms. Different strokes for… well, you know the old saying.

Is it wrong that I am considered a criminal for taking advantage of nature's two most powerful, beneficial and enjoyable products?

Is it wrong that I have spent most of my adult life, looking over my shoulder, simply because I enjoy temporarily altering my brain chemistry?

Is it wrong that people go to jail for doing exactly what I have done, only they've had the bad luck of getting caught?

You're goddamn right it's wrong. It's every kind of wrong!

Change needs to come and if enough of us demand it, then that change will come. And the world will be a better place, when it does.

There should be no stigma attached to taking drugs. We should all be free to discuss our drug intake, without fear. That's especially true, if your drug-taking is becoming problematic. Someone's health issue shouldn't also become a criminal issue and it's insane that we criminalise anyone for taking recreational drugs. People die sometimes, because they are afraid of arrest if they seek help.

It needs to stop. Now.

More than anything, this is a civil rights issue. Recreational drug users are treated like second class citizens. It's been said that this is the last major civil rights battle left to fight. Maybe that is true.

Disclosing to people that you're a recreational drug user, could be compared to the American military's former policy on homosexuality... Don't ask, don't tell. No one is asking and no one is telling.

185

Isn't it time we all stepped out of the green closet and told the truth? I want to tell, I want all of us who enjoy recreational drugs to speak up! We don't have to sit in the back of the bus any more. We count, we matter, we are no different to anyone else and it is time society started treating all of us better!

I reckon I have smoked around 20 kilos of weed in my lifetime, or around 44 pounds of it, if you prefer imperial measures. And that's a conservative estimate. I know that is a whole lot of weed. I don't have dain bramage (copyright everyone in the 70s) and haven't suffered any ill effects from this benign yet beneficial substance. We should all be free to ingest it.

And if I only do one decent thing with my life, I would like it to be that I did all I could to further this very important cause and helped bring it into the mainstream. We need to sort ourselves out as a society.

I started this book with a quote from Dr. Martin Luther King. He said that we all have a 'moral responsibility to disobey unjust laws'.

Drug laws are certainly that, they are completely unjust. Fighting this injustice is the most moral thing we can all do. Common sense and compassion need to prevail.

People may wonder who I am in real life, but in truth, it doesn't matter. If I told you my real name, it would be meaningless. I really am nobody. If you Googled my real name, you would find nothing.

Who is the northlondonhippy?

I am the northlondonhippy.

I'm a son, brother, a partner, a colleague, a friend, a blogger, a writer, a journalist, a fictional hippy and make-believe online drug activist and I take recreational drugs regularly and proudly.

I may be a nobody, but perhaps one day, I could be somebody. And maybe, just maybe, I am everybody who has ever taken drugs. And I'm giving the under-represented a loud voice that's rarely heard.

Nice people do take drugs, good people, people you know and perhaps people you may even love. We really are everywhere.

Who knows what the future holds for any of us. It has to get better, doesn't it?

Here's hoping all our futures will be green!

And as one of my favourite authors, Kurt Vonnegut, used to say: 'So it goes.'

And so do I.

— the northlondonhippy

About the author

The northlondonhippy is an anonymous blogger, online cannabis activist and recreational drug user, who has been writing about drugs and drug use, specifically his own, for over a decade. He has also worked in the media, mainly as a journalist, for 30 years.

Now based, unsurprisingly, in north London, the hippy hopes the punitive drug laws that have ripped families and society apart for decades, will soon be coming to an end.

Visit the northlondonhippy's website:

www.northlondonhippy.com

Follow the northlondonhippy on Twitter:

@nthlondonhippy

Appendix A
Select References & Sources

If you're interested in more information about some of the topics and subjects I've covered in the book, I've made a list of select references and sources, below. Where applicable, I have used links to Wikipedia. Where that's not an option, I've gone for the most authoritative and complete source available. Some chapters have been omitted, because they did not have any factual or historical references. I hope you find this useful.

Preface

Kurt Vonnegut quote: Taken from Deadeye Dick, Vonnegut's 1982 novel. Vonnegut is the hippy's favourite author
https://en.wikipedia.org/wiki/Deadeye_Dick

Martin Luther King Jr quote: Taken from Dr. King's open letter, written in 1963
https://en.wikipedia.org/wiki/Letter_from_Birmingham_Jail

Forward

The War on Drugs - The pointless 50-plus year pretend war on some people who use some drugs
https://en.wikipedia.org/wiki/War_on_Drugs

Alcohol Prohibition (USA) - Alcohol was banned for nearly 13 years. It didn't work and was overturned, but it did give birth to the Mafia
https://en.wikipedia.org/wiki/
Prohibition_in_the_United_States

Nice People Take Drugs campaign - Run by the campaign group, Release
http://www.release.org.uk/nice-people-take-drugs

Al Capone - US gangster who made his name, reputation and fortune thanks to alcohol prohibition
https://en.wikipedia.org/wiki/Al_Capone

Pablo Escobar - One of the most successful and wealthy drug traffickers ever, also one of the most violent. He wouldn't have existed without prohibition
https://en.wikipedia.org/wiki/Pablo_Escobar

Just say 'No' - A pointless and ineffective anti-drugs campaign spearheaded by former US First Lady, Nancy Reagan
https://en.wikipedia.org/wiki/Just_Say_No

President Richard M. Nixon - Former US President who launched the war on drugs in 1971 and the only US President to ever resign from office
https://en.wikipedia.org/wiki/Richard_Nixon

John Ehrlichman - One of Nixon's henchman, who said in an interview in 1994 that the war on drugs was used by Nixon to criminalise blacks and hippies http://edition.cnn.com/2016/03/23/politics/john-ehrlichman-richard-nixon-drug-war-blacks-hippie/

Canada legalisation - Prime Minister Justin Trudeau, campaigned for office with a pledge to legalise cannabis to keep young people safer. It is expected to happen soon.
https://en.wikipedia.org/wiki/
Legal_history_of_cannabis_in_Canada

Uruguay legalisation - The first country in the world to move towards a legalised and regulated market in cannabis
https://en.wikipedia.org/wiki/Cannabis_in_Uruguay

Professor David Nutt - Former head of the ACMD (Advisory Council on the Misuse of Drugs) and one of the world's leading experts on drugs. He was sacked by the UK government for making truthful, factual statements about drugs
https://en.wikipedia.org/wiki/David_Nutt

UK (Re)Classification - Cannabis was reclassified by Prime Minister Tony Blair's government, from Class B to C, then reclassified again by Blair's weak successor, Gordon Brown
https://en.wikipedia.org/wiki/
Cannabis_classification_in_the_United_Kingdom

Judge Francis Young - Administrative judge for the DEA (Drug Enforcement Administration) who ruled that cannabis is a safe and effective medication with no side effects
http://norml.org/news/2013/09/05/25-years-ago-dea-s-own-administrative-law-judge-ruled-cannabis-should-be-reclassified-under-federal-law

Professor Les Iversen - Current head of the UK's Advisory Council for the Misuse of Drugs (ACMD), who proclaimed cannabis safer than aspirin
http://www.independent.co.uk/life-style/health-and-families/health-news/cannabis-less-harmful-than-aspirin-says-scientist-634183.html

Chapter Three

Legal dispensaries - Shops in US states and other locations with medical or recreational cannabis programmes, staffed by budtenders that sell cannabis and cannabis products
https://en.wikipedia.org/wiki/Cannabis_shop

US states with medical cannabis programmes - Alaska, Arizona, California, Colorado, Connecticut, Delaware, Hawaii, Illinois, Maine, Maryland, Massachusetts, Michigan, Minnesota, Montana, Nevada, New Hampshire, New Jersey, New Mexico, New York, Ohio, Oregon, Pennsylvania, Rhode Island, Vermont, Washington (state), Washington DC (District of Colombia)
http://medicalmarijuana.procon.org/view.resource.php?resourceID=000881&print=true

US States with legal recreational cannabis - Alaska, Colorado, Oregon, Washington (state) & Washington DC (District of Colombia)
https://mic.com/articles/126303/where-is-marijuana-legal-in-the-united-states-list-of-recreational-and-medicinal-states#.IYgZawhXx

US States voting to legalise cannabis in 2016 - Arizona, California, Maine, Massachusetts and Nevada
http://www.fool.com/investing/2016/08/14/5-states-voting-on-recreational-marijuana-this-nov.aspx

Soviet/Afgan War - From 1979-1989. The US backed the Mujahideen, who eventually became the Taliban and Al Qaeda
https://en.wikipedia.org/wiki/Soviet–Afghan_War

Chapter Four

Dr Carl Hart - Professor of psychology and psychiatry at Columbia University. Dr. Hart is known for his research in drug abuse and drug addiction.
https://en.wikipedia.org/wiki/Carl_Hart

Dr Hart co-authored a letter to the Lancet, the UK's pre-eminent medical journal, calling them out for incorrectly linking cannabis directly to psychosis without evidence to substantiate the claim
http://hightimes.com/culture/scientists-call-out-bad-data-linking-weed-to-psychosis/

Chapter Five

Crack epidemic - Began in major US cities in the mid 1980s
https://en.wikipedia.org/wiki/Crack_epidemic

Crack vs Powdered Cocaine sentencing - Huge disparity in sentences for possession for these two different variants of the same drug, which was fixed by President Obama in 2010
https://en.wikipedia.org/wiki/Fair_Sentencing_Act

Chapter Seven

Rockefeller Drug Laws - Strict and punitive New York state drug laws, named after then governor & former Vice President, Nelson Rockefeller. Fun fact, he died shagging his secretary
https://en.wikipedia.org/wiki/Rockefeller_Drug_Laws

Chapter Eleven

Somalia famine 1992 - Which resulted in an aid relief program that brought US troops to the war torn country
https://en.wikipedia.org/wiki/Unified_Task_Force

Yugoslav Wars - Massive conflict in the mid 90s on European soil, that followed the break up of Yugoslavia
https://en.wikipedia.org/wiki/Yugoslav_Wars

Tuzla Air Base - Home of NATO peacekeepers in the 90s
https://en.wikipedia.org/wiki/Tuzla_Air_Base

Sierra Leone - The hippy spent a month hanging out here
https://en.wikipedia.org/wiki/Sierra_Leone

Bob Marley Night (Day) - Celebrated in Sierra Leone (and in other countries) on the 11th of May
http://www.sierraexpressmedia.com/?p=23672

Lockerbie bombers - Two Libyan nationals were tried in the Hague for the bombing of Pan Am flight 103. Questions about their involvement continue to this day
https://en.wikipedia.org/wiki/Pan_Am_Flight_103

Chapter Thirteen

Kurt Schmoke - Former mayor of Baltimore, who advocated decriminalising drugs in the 1980s, long before it was a mainstream idea
https://en.wikipedia.org/wiki/Kurt_Schmoke

US Opioid epidemic - An ongoing problem in the states today, deaths have been increasing
https://www.drugabuse.gov/about-nida/legislative-activities/testimony-to-congress/2016/americas-addiction-to-opioids-heroin-prescription-drug-abuse

Psychoactive Substance Bill (UK) - One of the dumbest laws ever drafted, utterly pointless. Meant to address legal highs/novel psychoactive substances, it has actually made the problem worse. Came into law in May 2016
http://www.drugwise.org.uk/wp-content/uploads/Psychoactive-SubstancesAct.pdf

Death of Princess Diana - The night Diana died in a car accident, while the hippy was under the influence of LSD
https://en.wikipedia.org/wiki/Death_of_Diana,_Princess_of_Wales

Chapter Twenty

Portugal - The first country to decriminalise all recreational drugs, in 2001. Seen universally as a resounding success
https://en.wikipedia.org/wiki/Drug_policy_of_Portugal

Colorado - First US state to legalise cannabis for recreational use. Also seen as a huge success
https://en.wikipedia.org/wiki/Cannabis_policy_of_Colorado

Privateer Holdings - One of the largest companies involved in the legal cannabis industry. Their subsidiaries including leafy.com - an excellent strain database. They also have the license to use Bob Marley's name for branding a strain of cannabis
https://en.wikipedia.org/wiki/Privateer_Holdings

London riots (2011) - Riots which engulfed London and other cities in the UK
https://en.wikipedia.org/wiki/2011_England_riots

Drug use is a basic human right - The hippy told you to Google this, but look, he did it for you already:
http://www.telegraph.co.uk/news/uknews/crime/11810347/Taking-drugs-is-a-human-right-say-MPs-and-peers.html

Maureen Dowd's edible disaster - New York Times reporter eats too much cannabis
http://www.nytimes.com/2014/06/04/opinion/dowd-dont-harsh-our-mellow-dude.html?_r=0

Chapter Twenty One

EDIT - everyonedoesit.com - One of the biggest online headshops in the world. The hippy had a partnership with them for the NLH Deluxe
http://www.everyonedoesit.com

RooR - One of the world's best glassware manufactures, who made the NLH Deluxe bong
http://roor.de

Noel Gallagher quote about drugs
http://www.independent.co.uk/news/drugs-are-like-a-cup-of-tea-says-noel-1285833.html

Chronic endocannabinoid deficiency - The hippy suffers from this
https://www.medicaljane.com/2013/11/08/cannabinoid-deficiency-may-explain-a-variety-of-health-conditions/

Magic mushroom research - To help people with end of life anxiety and depression. Extremely effective!
http://volteface.me/features/future-psychiatric-treatment-knocking/

Appendix B
Cannabis or Marijuana

Cannabis, also known as Marijuana, is a plant that has safely been used medicinally and recreationally for thousands of years,

Buds - The flowers of the female cannabis plant, which have the highest concentration of THC.

CBD - Cannabidiol - another of the many constituent chemicals in cannabis, which has anti-psychotic qualities. Not a controlled substance, you can legally purchase CBD oil for ingestion.

Dirt Weed - A term for commercially grown weed from the 70s and 80s. Known for being dry, brown, dusty and full of seeds. It was imported into the USA from Mexico or Colombia.

Entourage Effect - The combined action of all the constituent chemical components of Cannabis. Whole plant extracts are sought after for this reason.

Hybrid - A cannabis plant which has been crossbred between a Sativa and Indica. Can be dominant of one or the other, or 50/50 between the two.

Indica - One of the two main types of cannabis, Indica plants are shorter and stockier. The effects are more sedative like, which is known as 'couch lock'. An example would be a Kush, like Purple Kush.

Other names for Cannabis - Pot, weed, grass, ganja, dope, herb, reefer, Mary Jane, buds, nuggets, nugs, skunk, puff, and draw.

Sativa - The other main type of herbal cannabis, with taller plants that have skinnier leaves The effects are thought to be more uplifting and creative. It's known as a good day time smoke. An example would be a Haze, like Super Silver Haze.

Skunk (tabloid term) - As used by the UK media, a derogatory and factually incorrect catch-all tabloid term for cannabis grown domestically and poorly. Often finished prematurely, with lower CBD levels. Often all you can find in the UK.

Strains - The various "flavours" of cannabis, each with a different taste and psychoactive effect, with some better suited to different medical conditions, than others. Examples include some of the hippy's favourites, like Purple Kush, Chocolate Thai, Northern Lights or UK Cheese to name a few.

Super Skunk - One of the hippy's absolute favourite strains, potent, strong smelling and very enjoyable.

Terpenes - Essential oils contained in cannabis and other plants. Responsible for the odour and taste, thought to have some active qualities.

THC - Tetrahydrocannabinol - the main, psychoactive ingredient of Cannabis, which provides the high.

Trichomes - Fine hairs on a cannabis plant, which is where you would find the THC, CBD and terpenes. Also known as crystals or kief, these can be collected and made into hashish.

Appendix C
Cannabis growing and production

Cannabis is a plant, which grows wild all over the world.

Airbuds - The smaller, lower buds, which don't have as high a concentration of active chemicals. Can also be used to make hash and extracts.

Drying and curing - The process of turning the buds into something smokeable. After drying, the curing process matures the buds, providing a smoother, tastier smoke.

Flowering - The process of getting the plant to make THC-rich buds. For indoor plants, 12 hours of darkness and 12 hours of light, will induce this process.

Growth medium - Soil is the most basic form, but other types of medium can include cocoa and hydroponics.

Grow shops - Specialised stores which sell all the supplies you need to grow cannabis.

Hydroponics - Instead of using soil, a system of recirculating nutrient liquid is used. It is a cleaner way of growing indoors.

Indoor grows - Can be done under lights, with hydroponics instead of soil.

Leaves - These are like the solar panels of the plant, but have a very low concentration of THC and CBD.

Lights - There are various lights that can be used to grow weed. The most modern are LEDs, which use less electricity and don't get as hot.

Odour control - Carbon filters are used to take away the strong smell of cannabis as it is growing.

Outside grows - Cannabis will grow nearly anywhere, but to grow quality buds, you need a climate suited to the plant. Ideally, with lots of sunlight, decent soil and a good amount of rain,

Sexing - Telling the difference between male and female plants, before putting them into flower. Male plants can pollinate the females, which makes them go to seed, instead of flowering buds. You need to get rid of the male plants.

Sinsemilla - Female cannabis plants that have gone to flower.

Trim - The bits of the plant that are removed or trimmed, after harvesting. Can be used to make hash and other extracts.

Appendix D
Hashish, extracts & concentrates

Hashish, also known as hash, or solid, is an extraction of the active ingredients of the cannabis plant.

BHO - Butane Hash Oil - another name for dabs.

Charas and Indian Temple Ball - Two types of well known, hand collected hash from India.

Dabs - Cannabis extracts or concentrates, which are the purest forms of the drug. Taken by 'dabbing' a small amount on to a heated titanium nail, which turns it into a potent vapour. Can also be ingested via vape pens, which are similar to electronic cigarettes.

Kief - The crystals that come off of dried buds. Can be collected via dry sift over a wire mesh or you can buy a grinder that has a mesh in the base, with a chamber for collecting crystals.

Moroccan black - Also known as rocky, or sticky black. It's a hand collected, soft hash from Morocco.

Oil - Another solvent extract and type of dab, with an oily, viscous consistency. Can be taken via titanium nail, or dripped or painted on to a joint.

Production - dry sift - Dried buds are sifted with a wire mesh, the crystals are collected and pressed into hash. If it is not pressed, the loose crystals are often referred to as 'kief'.

Production - hand collected - The buds on living plants are massaged by hand until the plant oozes a sticky substance which is collected, pressed and made into hash. It's a traditional collection method and takes a lot of time.

Production - solvent extraction - Method is best suited to a laboratory, where the proper equipment can be used. The active ingredients are collected by blasting the plant with a solvent, like butane. The oil is collected, then the butane is purged, leaving a very potent extraction. The resulting product is known as a concentrate, such as wax, shatter, or oil. And all of them are known as dabs or BHO.

Production - water extraction - Ice cold water is used to snap the trichomes, which are then collected via a fine mesh in canvas bags, known as bubble bags. The crystals are then collected, dried, cured and pressed. This type of hash is often called ice-o-later or full melt.

Red Lebanese - Also known as red leb, it's made by dry sifting buds. Unsurprisingly, it comes from Lebanon.

Shatter - Another solvent extract and type of dab, which is clear, amber coloured and has the consistency of hard candy, like a lollypop.

Wax - A solvent extract and type of dab, which has been processed into a wax-like substance.

Appendix E
Cannabis Edibles

A cannabis edible is any food product which has been infused with the active ingredients of cannabis. The THC needs to be bonded with some sort of fat for your body to process it.

ABV - Already Been Vaped weed - if you use a vaporiser to ingest weed, the by-product is a slightly toasted weed, which has been decarboxylated already. Perfect for making cannabutter or infused oil.

Cannabis infused oil - I do this with coconut oil, which is solid at room temperature. Same process as cannabutter otherwise. Advantage is that coconut infused oil keeps longer, and is somewhat more versatile in cooking. Both oil and butter can be used in savoury or sweet foods.

Cannabutter - Butter infused with cannabis. Here's how I do it: Melt some butter in a slow cooker, add your ground cannabis (bud, trim, airbuds, even leaves work), then add hot water. Put the slow cooker on low for 6-8 hours or more, stirring occasionally. Pass the mixture through some cheesecloth to remove the plant matter, then put the remaining liquid in a bowl in your refrigerator. Leave for a few hours, or overnight and the butter will solidify and collect as a solid at the top of the bowl. Carefully remove the cannabutter, pat dry with kitchen towel and discard the remaining liquid. Use the cannabutter in any recipe that calls for normal butter, like brownies or cookies, Yum.

Decarboxylation - Is the process of heating the weed gently to turn the THCA into a form of active THC your body can more easily process. Some say this is a crucial step, but I don't always do it myself. Google will provide you with detailed instructions if you want to know more.

Dosage - Just a note on dosing with edibles. Always start small and wait a long time before having more. The effects of edibles are different from smoking, more intense and more long lasting. Be smart and be careful.

Space bars or space cake - Infused baked goods, a popular term for edibles in Holland.

Appendix F
Cannabis Paraphernalia

Bong - A pipe that cools the smoke by filtering it through water. Can be made of plastic, metal or glass, among other materials.

Bowl - Can refer to a pipe, or the part of a pipe or bong that holds the weed.

Doob tube - A straight glass tube that can hold a joint (or doobie) at the end, used for cooling the smoke.

EZ Widers - A popular US brand of rolling papers.

Joint - A cannabis cigarette, also known as a spliff, a zoot, or a doobie along with many other terms.

Pipes - A pipe used to smoke cannabis or hash. Can be made of any material, wood, ceramic, metal, stone, or glass.

Power hitter - A plastic squeezee bottle with a screw on cap, that holds a lit joint. Squeezing the bottle, forces air through the joint, creating a powerful flow of smoke.

Rizlas - The UK's most popular rolling papers.

Roach clip - An alligator clip used to hold the end of a joint, when it gets too small for your fingers.

RooR - northlondonhippy deluxe - A high end glass bong designed by the northlondonhippy, that was made by well known glassware manufacturer, RooR.

Vaporisers - A device that heats cannabis without burning the organic material, while turning the THC into vapour. A much safer, healthier way of enjoying cannabis.

Appendix G
Magic Mushrooms

Magic mushrooms are mushrooms which contain psilocybin, a psychedelic compound.

Copelandia Cyanescens - Also known as Hawaiian shrooms, a very potent strain, significantly more powerful than P. Cubes.

Dosage - Starter dose is 10 grams fresh, or 1 gram dry.

Grow Kit - Can come pre-inoculated with spores, or without. Easy to use, just add water and a bit of warmth.

Liberty Caps - The UK's most common magic mushroom, which grown wild around the country.

Psilocybe cubensis - Also known as P. Cubes. One of the most popular strains, sought after for their psychedelic properties.

Psilocybin - The active ingredient in magic mushrooms, which provides the psychedelic effects

Shrooms - Common slang for magic mushrooms.

Spores - The mushroom's reproductive units, which are used to grow mushrooms, including the magic variety.

Substrate - The growth medium used to cultivate mushrooms.

Appendix H
Other drugs

Benzodiazepines - Also known as benzos, a class of tranquillisers which include Valium (Diazepam) and Xanax. Highly addictive. **MDA** - Methylenedioxyamphetamine, known as the love drug in the 60s and 70s, a precursor of today's MDMA. A similar compound occurs naturally in nutmeg.

Cocaine - A powdered drug extracted from coca leaves, also known as Coke or Charlie. Euphoric and addictive.

Cocaine & Alcohol combination - Cocaethylene, which is manufactured in the liver, when both drugs are present in the blood stream. Makes the cocaine effects last longer, but has a higher toll on the user's heart.

Crack cocaine - A smokeable form of cocaine, sold and marketed as a cheap alternative to powdered cocaine. Popular from the mid 80s onwards, users are known as crackheads.

Crystal Methamphetamine (Meth) - A stronger, smokable form of speed, very addictive.

Fentanyl - A synthetic opioid which is 50 times stronger than heroin. It's responsible for an increasing number of overdoses, including Prince, the musician.

Heroin - A strong opiate, also known pharmacologically as diamorphine. A refined product from the opium poppy.

Heroin number 3 - Also known as brown, a smokeable form of heroin, some purer forms can be snorted or injected.

Heroin number 4 - A further refined product, also known as China White. Can be injected or snorted.

Ketamine - Known as Special K, another dissociative, popular from the 90s onwards as a club drug. Can cause bladder problems. Avoid.

MDMA - Methylenedioxymethamphetamine - also known as ecstasy, E, or Molly, popularised in the late 80s and early 90s, known for providing the user with euphoria and empathy. Used in psychotherapy and dance clubs. Was briefly hard to get.

LSD - Lysergic acid diethylamide, also known as Acid - a powerful psychedelic compound, with medical uses that are still being explored. Accidentally discovered by Albert Hofman.

Mescaline - A psychedelic drug which comes from Peyote Cactus, similar in effects to magic mushrooms and LSD.

PCP - Phencyclidine, also known as Angel Dust. An unpleasant dissociative, briefly popular in the 70s and 80s. Rumours of it being sprayed onto cannabis have proven unreliable.

Poly drug use - The use of two or more drugs at the same time, to achieve a desired effect.

Pure flake or fish scale cocaine - Marketing terms for cocaine which has not been cut, considered purer than standard powdered street cocaine.

Second golden age of MDMA - Happening now, after a brief period of unavailability. Variations of the drug currently available are more potent than before, and in great abundance.

Speed - Methamphetamine - an energetic drug that keeps users awake.

Appendix I
Legal highs/Novel Psychoactive Substances (NPS)

BZP - Benzylpiperazine - One of the first legal highs to have a psychoactive effect, slightly similar to MDMA. Used in farming as an anti-worming medication for animals.

Mephedrone - Also known as meph, M-Cat or Meow-Meow, another MDMA-like, formerly legal high.

Novel Psychoactive Substances - NPS, an increasingly popular class of drugs, with 2 or more launching each week in Europe. Popular because of the prohibition of all the good drugs, they are meant to mimic the effects of more well known recreational substances.

Synthetic cannabinoids - For example, JHW-18. Lab created compounds that have nothing in common with actual cannabis, but work on the same receptors in the brain. Avoid.

Whack weed - A legal cannabis substitute with no psychoactive effects that was popular in NYC in the 80s, used to con poor students in dodgy street deals.

Whippets/NO2 - Nitrous Oxide - a very safe drug that has been used for centuries, medically and recreationally. Medical uses include pain relief in dentistry and child birth.

Appendix J
For more information
Please visit the following sites:

They are all groups and causes supported by the northlondonhippy. 10% of all profits from this book, "Personal Use", will be donated to these charities.

Anyone's Child
http://anyoneschild.org

Anyone's Child: Families for Safer Drug Control is an international network of families whose lives have been wrecked by current drug laws and are now campaigning to change them. Young people will always use drugs. It's natural for them to experiment. 'Just say no' doesn't work, and neither does punishment. A criminal record for drug possession destroys a child's life, ruining job prospects, their status in society, and their futures. We believe that our drug laws need to properly protect our children. That's why we urgently need a new approach to keep all of our families safe. The next casualty of the drug war really could be Anyone's Child. Don't let it be yours.

The Beckley Foundation
http://beckleyfoundation.org

The Beckley Foundation's purpose is two-fold: 1) To scientifically investigate the effects of psychoactive substances on the brain and consciousness in order to harness their potential benefits and minimise their potential harms; learn more about consciousness and brain function; and discover and explore new avenues for the treatment of illnesses. 2) To achieve evidence-based changes in global drug policies in order to reduce the harms brought about by the unintended negative consequences of current drug policies; and develop improved policies based on health, harm reduction, cost-effectiveness, and human rights.

Drug Science (formerly the Independent Scientific Committee on Drugs)
http://www.drugscience.org.uk

Founded in 2010 by Professor David Nutt following his removal from post as Chair of the Advisory Council on the Misuse of Drugs, DrugScience is the only completely independent, science-led drugs charity, uniquely bringing together leading drugs experts from a wide range of specialisms to carry out groundbreaking original research into drug harms and effects. Its highly cited papers on all aspects of drug effects and harms attract global coverage and considerable public interest. DrugScience reduces the harms of drugs to the public through providing objective information on drug effects, harms and potential medical uses to the public, professionals and decision makers.

LEAP UK
http://ukleap.org
LEAP USA
http://www.leap.cc

LEAP stands for Law Enforcement Against Prohibition. They are a campaign group made up of former police, undercover operatives, intelligence service, military and a range of figures from the criminal justice system who have joined together with civilians to raise awareness to the failed, dangerous and expensive pursuit of a punitive drug policy.

Norml UK
http://norml-uk.org
Norml USA
http://norml.org

NORML is a non-partisan, non-profit organisation working for more research into the benefits of the uses of the cannabis plant for all purposes. They aim to provide a support network to those seeking the normalisation of cannabis consumption, and to influence a positive transformation of laws enabling responsible medical, spiritual, recreational and industrial uses in the UK.

Release
http://www.release.org.uk

Release is the national centre of expertise on drugs and drugs law. The organisation, founded in 1967, is an independent and registered charity.
The organisation campaigns directly on issues that impact on their clients - it is their experiences that drive the policy work that Release does and why they advocate for evidenced based drug policies that are founded on principles of public health rather than a criminal justice approach.

Support, Don't Punish
http://supportdontpunish.org

Support, Don't Punish is a global advocacy campaign calling for better drug policies that prioritise public health and human rights. The campaign aims to promote drug policy reform, and to change laws and policies which impede access to harm reduction interventions.

Transform
http://www.tdpf.org.uk

Transform is a charitable think tank that campaigns for the legal regulation of drugs both in the UK and internationally. Prohibition cannot be judged a success on any front. Handing control of the drug trade to organised criminals has had disastrous consequences across the globe. Transform therefore works to get drugs under control by advocating for strict regulation of all aspects of the trade.

Voltface
http://volteface.me

VolteFace is a policy innovation hub that explores alternatives to current public policies relating to drugs. They cultivate fresh thinking and new ideas via our online and print magazine and an ongoing programme of private and public events. They cover the policy and politics of drugs from the perspectives of science, health, lifestyle, culture, business and economics. VolteFace are UK-based and focussed whilst engaging with ideas and practice from across the world.

Political parties in the UK that support drug law reform:

CISTA UK
http://cista.org

Cannabis is Safer Than Alcohol (CISTA) is a political party in the UK who are campaigning on a single issue, to reform and improve our laws regarding cannabis.

Green Party
https://www.greenparty.org.uk

The Green Party have a lot of common sense policies that would benefit our society, including reforming our cannabis and drug laws in the UK.

The Liberal Democrats
http://www.libdems.org.uk

The Liberal Democrats became the first political party to support a regulated cannabis market in the UK today. The party commissioned a groundbreaking report into how a regulated cannabis market could work in the UK. This expert report was produced by a panel comprised of police officers, public health experts and drugs policy analysts.

Write your MP and demand they change the laws!

Special mention:

UK Cannabis Social Clubs
http://ukcsc.co.uk/

The UKCSC is an NGO platform founded in 2011 by citizens throughout the United Kingdom affected by and/ or concerned by the current national and international war on people who use certain drugs, particularly cannabis. UKCSC unites the representatives of individual CSC's in the UK, health workers, industry professionals, experts, entrepreneurs and activists from across not only the UK but Europe and the rest of the world.

Erowid
erowid.org

And finally, for unbiased information about recreational drugs, Erowid is one of the best resources online.

Special Thanks

Mrs Hippy - for always being there and putting up with me

Bob Scare - you couldn't ask for a better, best friend

Julian D - for copy editing this manuscript & fixing all my ~~tpyos~~ typos

John C - for reading the rough draft & providing really helpful feedback

And finally, to all of you, who have read this book. Thank you for using some of your valuable time by reading the words that I've written.

#0153 - 141116 - C0 - 210/148/12 - PB - DID1649679